A Special Thanks

Thank you so much for purchasing my book! I hope you will enjoy the learning journey we're about to embark on!

To show you my gratitude, I created a FREE downloadable booklet about the three main teaching theories. These theories are the pillar on which modern education lies, therefore they contain essential knowledge for aspiring teachers.

Visit www.gunstevenson.com to download your FREE "Essential Teaching Theories Booklet!"

The Art of Effective Teaching

Balance Different Learning Needs.
Communicate with Clarity. Motivate, Engage,
and Empower.

By Gunnar Stevenson

Table of Contents

8

Introduction

Back when I was just starting out as an assistant professor, I made a pretty significant error on the syllabus for the course I was teaching. I had arranged the course grading in a way that students earned points for each assignment, and at the end of the semester, everyone would receive a letter grade based on how many points they had earned. Math has never been my strong suit, and I don't pretend to find complicated formulas and equations easy. (Making this confession to you as a former engineer requires some courage.) The truth is, I should have caught this very simple addition error on my syllabus. Somehow, I had so many assignments and quizzes, students were able to acquire enough points prior to the end of term to earn As and Bs for the course without completing the final examination. Some exceptional students had even been able to stop completing assignments altogether in the final month of the semester.

As a result of my calculation error, many students who crossed the threshold of the grade they wanted stopped coming to class, so attendance in my course dwindled. There were fewer and fewer students each class period, and only those students who struggled and still needed points to get an A would come. For the final test only the worst performers showed up. If I'm trying to be an optimist here, I could argue that due to this error I could devote more time to the low-performing students. But the reality was, losing out on the brighter students driving much of the in-class participation had a major negative impact. Class sessions really benefitted from participation from both high- and low-achieving groups of students.

It was clear that the misjudgment in grading calculation was mine, and that I had created more assignments for my class, but not gone back to the points required to earn a particular letter grade and adjusted those numbers accordingly. I learned a lesson thanks to this experience; ever since then I double and triple-checked my syllabi to ensure I didn't lose half the class at the end of a semester, and docked points for students who missed class.

This was the beginning of an ongoing list of information I have learned over my many years of teaching. But not the last. Over time, my list of notes became a resource I used many times during my career and essentially self-taught myself how to teach effectively. That ominous semester I learned another important lesson. My classes were not interesting and engaging enough for my students to attend them despite already earning a top grade. There was work to be done in that department, too. What did I do wrong? How could I make my classes more captivating? How could I trigger passion in the hearts of my students about a subject they didn't naturally feel strongly about? I took these questions very seriously over the course of the years. When I retired, I was blessed to receive an acknowledgement for being one of the teachers with the highest class attendance.

This brings us to the purpose of this book, which is to help anyone tap into the resources and techniques I have learned over my career and show others how to develop their teaching abilities and apply them in virtually any setting.

Nearly all parents in the US, Canada, and Europe have been forced to become teachers in one way or another. Pre-COVID19, the most parents had to do was help their children with homework, explain difficult concepts and review multiplication tables. Some parents went as far as to teach through practical lessons such as explaining the chemical reactions that occur in baking, for instance. In this situation, a parent might decide to bake a few cakes, then select baking soda as a leavening agent for one and an equal amount of baking powder as the leavening ingredient for the other. When the cakes have fully cooked, the parent and child will compare the differences in the cakes and explain the chemical reactions.

The dynamic of teaching and how and where children learn has changed dramatically in a post-COVID19 world. Many schools, K-12 and universities, have opted to teach online, and that has had both positive and negative outcomes. Many parents have become de facto teachers in the wake of COVID, which puts an extra burden on the top of an already impossible situation. This has impacted my own family, as my youngest grandchild started third grade this year. I am saddened to say he hates it. Much of his learning takes place with little to no social interaction, and because his lessons are online, he has few tactile experiences that allow him to learn concepts in ways other than video lecture. Luckily, teaching is my passion and my recent retirement means I can help create a variety of lessons to enhance his schoolteacher's assignments. Plus, it's just much more fun to learn fractions with the broken segments of a Hershey's Chocolate Bar, since you get to snack on the pieces when you're done.

Whether you are a parent who has been thrust into learning "new math" in an effort to teach your children, are a dedicated homeschooler, or someone who works in organizational development at your company, training staff on new equipment or policies or giving professional development workshops, this book is designed to help you become a more engaged and effective teacher. Zoom is an amazing service that has enabled many people to both teach and work from home, but it has its limitations. There are fewer opportunities for group work and brainstorming. Tuning out of a meeting and working on other tasks is far too easy, especially when a participant turns off his or her microphone.

The lesson I learned as a young professor about triple-checking my syllabi for errors is but one of many lessons I have been taught in all my years of teaching. I aim to share all I have learned with you so you, too, can be an inspiring and effective teacher. Students learn more and are more engaged in the material when the instructor is knowledgeable and confident in their role and able to deliver information in a variety of ways.

The fact that many people learn differently is commonly known, but we rarely talk about how teachers meet the needs of students with differing learning styles. This book will help you develop a colorful palette of teaching skills to apply to a variety of students, and will bring out your inner teacher.

Chapter 1: What Makes a Good Teacher

Take a moment to think back to your days in school. It can be any level of education, elementary school, high school, or higher education. Sift through your memories and think about your favorite teacher. Who was he or she and what made this person your favorite teacher? Now think about the worst teacher you ever had in school. Did she hand out detentions like they were candy? Did he talk down to all the students, telling them they were stupid and wouldn't amount to much? What made this teacher so bad?

In my own experience, it takes about fifteen seconds to remember my favorite teacher. Her name was Mrs. Stegall, and she taught me in fifth grade. It was her kindness for her students that I will never forget. She always asked us as a class, "Who loves you?" and the class would respond in unison, "Mrs. Stegall." Up to this point in my life, I had nice teachers and mean teachers, but I cannot recall, before or since, any teacher ever expressing love for me as a student. The expression of genuine caring and love clearly meant something to me as out of all the teachers I have had, she is one I will never forget.

Interestingly, I know I am not the only student she had such a profound effect on. The last time I visited my hometown, I had a chance meeting with the mother of one of my schoolmates. Aaron and I gone to school together since childhood, and he'd had Mrs. Stegall for fifth grade too. I don't recall ever having spoken to Aaron's mother about Mrs. Stegall and how she'd had such a profound impact on my life, but during our brief conversation, Aaron's mother asked me if I was aware Mrs. Stegall had died. I had not been aware, and Aaron's mother told me about how, after retiring from teaching, Mrs. Stegall had become a naturopath for many years. By the way she spoke, I felt certain Aaron had been a big fan of Mrs. Stegall too.

What are the qualities that made Mrs. Stegall and your own favorite teacher so amazing at their job? Maybe this person spent extra time with you because you struggled in a particular subject or with a difficult concept. Maybe the way this person taught a certain subject inspired you to choose your career or area of research to study. I bet you enjoyed their lessons as they were probably engaging, and your teacher graded fairly too. Guess what? The research agrees with you. Many of these types of qualities are what make a teacher great. Let's dive into it and see what it takes to adopt some of these attributes.

The Habits and Traits of Good Teachers

One of my favorite books about the trials and tribulations of teaching is *Miss Nelson Is Missing* by Harry Allard and James Marshall. This beloved children's book tells the story of the sweet and kind Miss Nelson and the naughty, rude children in her classroom. One day, Miss Nelson gets fed up with how the class treats her and doesn't come to school. Her substitute is Miss Viola Swamp, and she is strict and mean. After a few days of being taught by Miss Swamp, the children begin to miss Miss Nelson terribly and investigate her whereabouts. Just as the naughty children have given up all hope Miss Nelson will return, she reappears, and the children are so grateful to have her back they no longer misbehave or treat her poorly. At the end of the book, Miss Nelson is at home in her bedroom, reminiscing about her day and how well-behaved the children were, when we get to peek into her closet to see the ugly black dress and black wig that had been worn by Miss Swamp.

Is Miss Nelson a good teacher or a bad teacher? That's somewhat debatable as this story presents both positive and negative qualities of Miss Nelson's teaching style. On one hand, the children like her and she's very personable. One of the primary qualities that lends itself to a good teaching and learning experience is a positive student-teacher relationship.[i] Without this relationship, we see the breakdown of the educational experience. While the children in our story were well-behaved under the thumb of Miss Swamp, they disliked school and yearned for the positivity Miss Nelson brought into the classroom each day.

Whether you are teaching your own children by supporting their distance learning, homeschooling, or training adults, think about how you would feel if your boss was constantly criticizing your work or never said thank you when you went above and beyond for the company. Would you want to continue to work for this company? Unless there were some outstanding perks, you would likely look for a new job where you would feel valued and appreciated. Students share the same feeling. Harsh critique and an educator who isn't patient or fair is probably going to instill a distaste for learning that can last a lifetime. [ii]

Here, I would like to make an important distinction between being strict but fair and being strict to intimidate. Strict but honest and fair teachers are usually well-respected and loved by students. Even if they would never admit it, most students are grateful for not-so-pleasant-to-hear feedback as long as it's delivered with care and the intention to help. A student who becomes more successful and accomplished thanks to kind but critical feedback usually will think of the teacher positively. On the other hand, strict teachers who use shaming, blaming, and intimidation as weapons may get a more compliant classroom, but they will be disliked and whatever they teach won't stick as well in their students' minds.

Let me present a recent activity I helped Ethan, my grandson, complete. In this assignment Ethan needed to write a short story about a fictional character. The purpose of the assignment was really to review the different parts of a story: the exposition, rising action, climax, falling action, and resolution. Right away, Ethan begins telling me the story he is going to write about. The more he tells me, the more I realize the story sounds familiar and perhaps I have read it in a book or seen it in a movie. When I ask Ethan about where he came up with the ideas for his story, he says he just made them up. The more I think about it,

I realize he's telling me the plot to Disney's *Coco*.

When this happened, I could have reacted negatively to Ethan's childish dishonesty and scolded him for trying to pass someone else's work off as his own. But instead, I decided to have a conversation with him. I mentioned to Ethan that his story sounded a lot like the movie *Coco*, and Ethan thought about it for a minute and agreed his story was similar to the movie we had watched together a few weeks earlier. I asked him if he would want someone to take his ideas and pretend they had come up with them. Ethan agreed he would not find that acceptable.

From there, I began to ask Ethan how he might come up with his own character. What was it about Miguel that Ethan found so likeable to make him the main character? Ethan responded that Miguel wanted to be a guitar player, and he went through the Land of the Dead to find his father. I proposed we create a character with similar passions. Through reviewing what Ethan liked about *Coco*, Ethan learned to write out the different parts of his story, but to do so originally, by coming up with his own characters and their own journey for the story.

Do you think the outcome would have been the same if Ethan had written his story and when I read it, I ripped up the pages he had written and called him a cheater for copying another person's idea? Probably not; in fact he likely would have lost all passion for the activity the second I ripped his story apart. Educators need to think about how to encourage and support their students, not tear them down. This creates a safe environment for people to learn and know it's okay to make mistakes because they won't be made fun of or punished for doing so.[iii]

Another thing to consider is the expectations you have for your students. One of the most amazing things I learned in all my years of teaching is that if you expect great things from those you teach, many will strive not to disappoint. [iv] As an educator, part of your job goes well beyond presenting material and the opportunity to learn. *It includes setting forth what you expect from your students in terms of their performance.* If you set the bar low, that is what you will get, and I think the year I taught the course with the rotten syllabus makes that clear. Once students had gotten what they felt they needed from my course, the desired letter grade, they quit. However, if you set the bar high, students will aim to excel and reach that goal, not necessarily to impress you, but because it's important to them to achieve greatness. Be there to show your students you care and are proud of their achievements.

I'd like you to conjure up the image in your mind of a typical absent-minded professor. What does this person look like, but more importantly, does he do his job well? I always imagine the absent-minded professor as looking something like Albert Einstein with his wild hair and big bushy mustache. I envision him shuffling to class in disheveled clothing with papers sticking out of his briefcase in every direction. When he tries to return the papers to the students, he calls out several names only to then realize he brought the papers for the wrong class. When the students do finally get their papers back, they have been stained with coffee and food and the only feedback is the numerical or letter grade in the hated red ink. His lessons always seem incomplete and he spends an inordinate amount of time fiddling with the computer setup for his slides. He rarely gets to complete a lecture before the class period ends. He is hardly an effective teacher.

In comparison, imagine a teacher who is organized and prepared for class. Not only does he look the part with a neat appearance and well-arranged materials, but his students receive timely, effective, personalized feedback on their assignments so that they can improve their study habits or adjust how they write their papers for future assignments. When the students enter the classroom, the professor sets up his slides and lecture quickly and takes care of any needed business efficiently before the lecture starts. "Don't forget you have a paper due next Tuesday," he might say. This professor's lectures are thought out, fun, engaging, and leave time for students to ask questions and actively participate in the material. He knows how his students are performing, checks in with them throughout the semester, and volunteers to help those who struggle with the material.

I'm sure you've likely heard the common expression *failing to plan is a plan for failure*. I've just presented two completely different teachers and teaching styles. And trust me, these archetypes exist at all levels of education.

As you begin to take on the role of educator in your home, company, or community, what style do you want to emulate? Grab a pen and paper, and write it down. How would you like to show up as a teacher? What would be your top three goals? How can you make sure you achieve these objectives? What do you think are your *weaknesses* as an educator? Are they meaningful? Do they prevent you from achieving your teaching goals? If yes, how can you improve in those areas? Take some time to really think about these questions. These are your route to becoming who you hope to be as a teacher. You have the power to become just the educator you'd like to be. Everything you need is already within you.

Being organized and prepared not only helps you be a more effective teacher, but it also helps your students learn better.[v,vi,vii] In this case, when you aren't prepared and organized, it is your actions that put students at risk for not succeeding. Think about your lessons and what you want them to cover. What are the most important topics and how can you review them in an engaging way? Additionally, make sure you are well-versed in what you are teaching [viii]. Students will know when you are not experienced with the subject matter at hand and lose confidence in your abilities. You can become both a teacher and a learner if you are jumping into a new area of teaching. Don't be afraid to take on both roles.

And last, but most certainly not least, love what you do! [ix,x,xi] Not everyone is cut out to teach in a classroom setting, but nearly everyone can take on the role of an educator. Whether it is teaching your infant daughter to take her first steps or murmur her first words or sharing tips and tricks on how to style hair and makeup by creating video tutorials on YouTube, you have taught someone something. When you are really passionate about what you are teaching, it shows. That passion and drive is communicated in the time and effort you put into your teaching. When you let your joy for teaching take over, your students will know it by the quality of your lessons. So take the time to revel in those moments and share your knowledge with others.

Let's repeat the "who was your favorite teacher" activity we did at the beginning of this chapter, except this time, imagine yourself in the role of that teacher. What does that look like to you? Of the qualities and habits presented in this chapter, which ones will be easy for you to adopt and why? Which habits might be more challenging? If your students become difficult like the children in *Miss Nelson Is Missing*, how will you respond? How do you picture the ideal learning environment for you and those you educate? Know that teaching is a little bit of trial by fire, no matter how much planning and preparation you put into it. No two students or classes will be the same, and you will need to adjust accordingly. The important piece is that if you are ready for the challenge of educating others and can motivate those you teach to put the effort in and learn, you'll catch your stride and succeed.

Chapter 2: What Motivates Students?

When I originally enrolled in college to study mechanical engineering, I entered as a pre-med student. I had great aspirations to become a surgeon and improve the lives of others. However, as I took classes that were prerequisites for upper-level courses, I didn't have the drive or interest to do well in them. I struggled in courses like microbiology, anatomy and physiology, and the math was more than I cared to handle. I despised the labs for these classes, slept through a majority of the lectures, and completely abandoned my lab partners in anatomy and physiology lab when we began dissecting a cat. That semester was my last semester in pre-med. Not only was I destined never to make it into medical school with the 1.85 GPA I earned that term, I knew beyond a shadow of a doubt being a surgeon was not my dream. It had been some else's.

As a young boy, my parents had always stressed the importance of education, and just like most parents, mine wanted me to do better in life than they had. To my parents, that meant going to college and becoming a doctor or lawyer or maybe an engineer. My parents placed a high value on the importance of getting into an American university and the life of success an American degree would bring. The only problem was that I hated the classes and the material so much I was sabotaging my own success. When I found out the lab instructor for my microbiology lab's three-month-long case of strep throat was actually caused by a chronic E. coli infection, I was out. That was the straw that broke the camel's back.

What followed was a serious reflection of the subjects and areas I enjoyed, and conversations with professors in those areas who could help guide me on my way to potential careers. Many of these careers held my interest, and I considered several of them in the years leading up to my graduation with my bachelor's degree. When it became time to make some decisions in the fall semester of my senior year, I decided on graduate school with my goal being entering the professoriate. And my parents, while they had stressed particular careers and areas of study, were just as happy to have me be successful in another field. It was important to both them and me that I find happiness in a career that motivated and inspired me to achieve.

In this chapter, we'll take a look at the importance of considering motivation from the student's perspective. In the last chapter we delved into what we look for in our ideal teacher, but now I want you to think about your ideal student. In a perfect world every person you worked with would be enthusiastic and ready to learn. Their mind would be a sponge, prepared to soak up all the knowledge and expertise you have to share. There would be no cajoling. You wouldn't need to leverage the threat of earning a bad grade to prompt them to show mastery of their knowledge. In fact, the relationship with this student might be more of a mentor/mentee relationship, where you, as the instructor, also learn through mutually exploratory conversations and research.

Sadly, you won't always have that experience with students. Some students will be motivated to learn only to earn grades that please their parents and allow them certain privileges after their report card is sent home every quarter. When my son was in grade school, he had a classmate whose parents paid him money for his grades.

Ten dollars for every A, five dollars for every B, and two for every C.

Other students you'll encounter won't have any motivation to learn at all. They find school to be a waste of time, and they simply attend because it is a mandate set forth by their parents. Some of those parents may also have such little value for education that only the threat of a visit from the truancy officer keeps the child in school.

So how can you know what motivates each student? Well, you can't. At least not instantly. It takes time to build a personal relationship with your pupils. Learning what drives each person is just one of the many reasons the student-instructor relationship is so powerful. There can be any number of variables affecting motivation, but one of the primary ones is the *fear of failure*.

The fear of failure is something that you can find in students of any age. And it's not something only shy students experience. Anytime a person stretches the limits of their knowledge and looks to undertake something new, there is a risk of failing. As an educator, it's important to remember that while failure is not an option, it is a natural part of the learning process.

In 1997 Nike aired a commercial featuring Michael Jordan reviewing a laundry list of his failures.[xii] Michael, arguably one the best professional basketball players of all-time, tells the viewer how he has missed over 9,000 shots, been on the losing team more than 300 times, and personally missed what would have been game-winning goals for his team at least 26 times. Michael then tells us that these failures were what made him successful. His motivation and compulsive drive to be the absolute best has personally led to him to six championships, five MVP awards, and the title of best defender of all time.[xiii] It is Jordan's willingness to get back on the court after a poor showing that has allowed him to continue playing and achieve such a level of greatness.

There is no doubt that Michael Jordan is one legendary NBA player. Even people who don't follow the sport see a black and red Chicago Bulls basketball jersey with the number 23 and instantly think of Jordan and all his successes. But here, we have a sports idol telling us that if it weren't for his failures, he never would have succeeded. If Michael Jordan had quit basketball the first time he missed a basket or lost a game or when he was cut from his sophomore team in high school, the world would have been robbed of his talent and its impact. Little boys and girls wouldn't have idolized him and worked hard to achieve their own goals, and our world would have likely been poorer of their talent as well. In the 2017 playoff game between the Cleveland Cavaliers and Boston Celtics, LeBron James surpassed Michael Jordan's count of 5,987 post-season points.[xiv] In a post-game interview, James specifically cited Jordan as being the reason he began playing basketball and the inspiration that cemented his love for the game. This is important to acknowledge because it illustrates the ripples of impact one's failures and achievements can have long down the road.

Failure and wrong answers aren't to be shamed or used to make a learner doubt their ability. In fact, quite the opposite: both the educator and learner should view errors and mistakes as opportunities to grow and further develop the requisite knowledge and skills. As an educator, help your students see this. Be aware that instructors who belittle the student after a failure will stamp out the desire to learn faster than anything else in this world. If you tell a person he or she is inadequate and too stupid to ever learn something or make fun of a person for a simple error, don't be surprised if that criticism becomes a self-fulfilling prophecy. No wonder bullying is such an issue these days.

We'll discuss difficult students in a later chapter, but it's important to reflect on your behavior to ensure it is not the source of the problem. Remember, students aren't all cut from the same cloth. You might need to vary your teaching style to meet the needs of your learner. An example might be a personal trainer with two different clients. Client A may be motivated by an upcoming event, like a wedding, and prefer his or her trainer to really get into the exercises with them. So when the trainer yells, "Amy, keep going! You're going to look great in that wedding dress," that may work great for Client A—but it may be a huge problem for Client B, who doesn't want any extra attention drawn to him. He is just working out with a trainer to lose the few pounds he gained during quarantine.

Intrinsic and Extrinsic Motivation

In addition to a wide and varying range of motivations for students, there are also different *sources* for motivation. Extrinsic motivation flares up from an outside source, such as the need to eat and pay rent being the motivation for holding a steady job. On the other hand, intrinsic motivation comes from within.[xv] My intrinsic desire to breed and raise English Springer Spaniels, for example, is due to my undying love for the breed.

When we think about intrinsic and extrinsic motivation in a learner/educator situation, the concepts apply differently to children versus adults. Often, the things children are compelled to learn are thrust upon them by schools, parents, and supervisors (for older children who work), and they get little choice in what they are taught and the methodology used. Much of the motivation here is extrinsic, and while lessons can be designed to be fun and not feel like a chore, the motivation to learn is still being pushed upon the child by an outside force.

Adults, however, get a lot more freedom in selecting what they learn and how. From higher education to personal hobbies, adults are given more control, and therefore more of the student's motivation comes from an internal source. While nearly all four-year college degrees require a certain number of general education courses that are, presumably, meeting particular requirements across numerous university curricula, students often have the option to choose any two science, any two math, and any two language and composition courses. While one student may be satisfied with a basic Biology 101 type of course, some students may take a course specifically on bee biology, for example, simply because they find the subject matter interesting and fun.

As adults, we can choose to spend our money and time any way we wish. If we want to learn a new hobby, even one that is costly, like golf or learning a musical instrument, we can choose to do so with little input from others. Some children may get the option to choose their post-school interests. Others may be limited by their parents' finances and values. When I was in primary school, my parents paid for me to take piano lessons in our small town. When I had been taking lessons for five or six years I no longer wanted to continue, but my parents insisted I stick with it. I did as they instructed but today, I could not likely play more than a few notes of any song, as I really had no passion for the instrument.

I find it important to keep the difference between extrinsic and intrinsic motivation in mind while teaching. When we want to spark interest toward our subject in a child who was clearly externally forced to attend our classes, we need to use empathy, first and foremost. To some it can mean a lot if we genuinely assure them that we know attending our class may feel like a chore. The kid will probably agree. The next step is to get to know this student a bit, get interested in what he likes. So just ask, "What would you like to do/ to learn instead?" After some—usually sweet—pouting, they the child will tell us what they actually like. This is the moment when we need to use our creativity skill—and we need to use it fast. How can we tie together our material with the interest of the child? Let's say you teach English literature and grammar. If the student said they wanted to be wizards like Harry Potter, for example, you can tell them that the author of *Harry Potter*, J.K. Rowling, was able to write such a great story because she was very active in

English literature and grammar class. While this won't turn anyone into a wizard, words certainly hold some magic in them.

This "trick" works with every age group. Of course, you need to tailor your example to your student's needs. If you need to engage a teenager, a contemporary "cool" reference can work well. In case of adults, bring up a role model who excels in the field you're teaching about and tie it with the ultimate goal of the adult student.

Bottom line, try to tap into the intrinsic motivations of your students and connect them to the sometimes unavoidable and undesired extrinsic motivation they carry.

How to Encourage Intrinsic Motivation?

Think back to the beginning of this chapter, where we described our ideal student; someone driven to learn due to an unquenchable thirst for the knowledge you have to share. That is the student we all want to teach. But few of the students who come our way will actually be those magical unicorns we yearn to educate and develop into another person who is just as thrilled by learning to create a plasma from items around our home to sanitize N-95 masks in our microwave as we are.[xvi] Yes, you can actually do this, and yes, there will be a fire inside your microwave, but that's supposed to happen. In any case, don't try it at home on my account.

So how do we encourage and increase a learner's intrinsic motivation?

<u>Freedom of Choice aka Autonomy</u>: [xvii,xviii] Giving someone a choice in what they learn can go a long way in tapping into their internal motivation reservoir. We've already explored this somewhat, but it can include more than just

our subject material. Think about providing students with the freedom of choice in selecting which learning style fits them best. When students can choose between a visual, auditory, or tactile approach, they will instinctively select the style that is easiest for them to work with and understand. This can be especially helpful when working with those who have learning disabilities. They will gain confidence in themselves as students, and they will like your subject more and more as they become successful in a learning environment.

Give an A for Effort:[xix] With younger children, it's important to acknowledge their willingness to put themselves out there with such enthusiasm and joy. Even if a child gets an answer wrong, praise them for putting in the effort it took to dare answering the question. Then review where they went wrong and correct their error to put them back on the right path. This can be done one on one, in small groups, or even in a larger group where respectful limitations are set.

Get Your Students' Attention by Engaging Their Interest:[xx, xxi] Make the material you are delivering interesting to those you teach. One of my good friends and colleagues, William, is a professor of English history. I recall his joy when he discovered that one of his dry and rather boring lectures had a couple really active students in it. They asked questions, had good discussions, and the learning environment was exciting for William because the students weren't just staring at him with glazed eyes and half asleep. Why were these students so interested in this course? William's class focused on the Middle Ages and the movie *Braveheart* would often become a topic of discussion. The students followed William's lectures along in the lineage of English rule up to Edward II, dispelled a few myths about the film and the legendary William Wallace, and continued right on through the Hundred Years War and the Black Prince.

The movie *Braveheart* was what had stoked an interest in these students to learn more about English history. William used this observation in future semesters to create more engaging classes that students participated in and enjoyed. One year he developed a special topics course that focused on English history through movies. He showed films like *Elizabeth* (1998), *Braveheart, Lady Jane,* and other similar ones. I thought William's idea of using popular culture to teach his subject material was brilliant. When the BBC released *The Hollow Crown* in 2012, showcasing some of today's biggest stars like Benedict Cumberbatch, Tom Hiddleston, Jeremy Irons, and Ben Whishaw, all known to American audiences through big-budget films, I thought it would be a great opportunity for someone who teaches Shakespeare. Now that features like

Hamilton can be seen on Disney+, the opportunities are endless, and a teacher can use literature, magazines, news articles, or even true crime to engage and interest their students in a variety of different subjects.

Why Do I Need to Know *This*? [xxii] It's important for students to understand, especially as they get older, why they are learning all this information you are sharing with them. You can teach a student how to calculate the degrees of each angle of an isosceles triangle, but is that something they *really* need to know? Will they ever use that in the real world? Well, yes, it could be that your students will use this information on a regular basis. Isosceles triangles are used in architecture, graphic design, in the study of cubic equations and celestial mechanics, and are even used as religious or mystical symbols. So, there are actually quite a few real-life applications, from anthropology to cultural studies, astronomy, algebra, and design and architecture, where this information is relevant and useful. If you can communicate that to your students, those who are interested in those areas will be much more likely to tune in and pay attention.

Experiential Education:[xxiii] The concept of Experiential Education comes from the book *Flow: The Psychology of Optimal Experience* by Mihaly Csikszentmihalyi. The primary premise behind the "flow" experience involves matching up a student's skill level with a correlating activity and performance expectation. If the student is matched to a task that is too easy, such as asking a James Beard Award-winning chef to spend the day chopping vegetables, the student won't be challenged and will subsequently disengage from learning due to disinterest. On the other hand, if the task is too difficult, such as conducting an elaborate and precise chemistry experiment for a student who has never stepped foot in a science lab, the student is likely to have anxiety and a decreased sense of self-worth. Those feelings can lead the student into a cycle of negative reinforcement that can have a lifelong impact on their desire and willingness to learn.

When the student and activity are harmoniously matched, it creates a positive feeling of engagement that, along with culturally aware teaching techniques, increases the student's intrinsic motivation. When combined with the autonomy to engage in a variety of learning styles, which can help meet the needs of students who don't learn well in traditional environments, the setting is ripe for encouraging individual motivation from within. Once the student experiences positive student-driven learning experiences, their internal motivation increases along with a desire to learn more.

In this recipe for learning success, we have our equipment: educators and learners. We've discussed what our ideal traits and qualities are in each of these groups, and we've identified some important factors related to understanding and encouraging student motivation, as well as understanding the mistakes we can make as educators that lead students to disengage from the learning process. Now we need some ingredients, and by far the most important one is communication. In our next chapter, we'll delve into why teaching with clarity is so crucial to learning.

Chapter 3: Clear Communication

When my son was about two years old, his mother and I put him down to bed and then decided to watch a movie together as it was still early in the evening. As David was so young, all his television experience revolved around cartoon movies or television shows, things that were appropriate for a child of his age. Well, David, the curious little monster that he was, decided to pay his mom and me a visit in the living room to ask, "Whatchya watching?"

Surprised to see him there, during what was a big and bloody battle scene of some action movie, I blurted out, "An adult movie." I followed this quickly with, "Don't ever repeat that." I had just informed my two-year-old I was watching an "adult movie" with his mother. While he would be unlikely to remember it, I would definitely never forget the mortification involved should he decide to share this newfound knowledge with anyone else, like his grandparents or the nursery-school teacher who watched him during the day. While I realized the error of my words the second they had escaped my mouth, sometimes it's not so easy to recognize where your communication with others has gone wrong.

What Does It Mean to Teach?

In my haste to quickly answer my son's question and usher him out of the room, I had responded to a simple question in a way that was unclear and confusing. It should come as no surprise that teachers can and often do teach in ways that are confusing to some students. That's why it's so important to understand and acknowledge what teaching means to us as educators. We each have an internal metaphor of how we conceptualize and plan to realize our thoughts and opinions on how we work with students. Do we see ourselves as a quirky and cool yet adventuresome Ms. Frizzle type from *The Magic School Bus* series? Or rather an inspirational professor who encourages her students to live their lives to the fullest and make every day extraordinary, like Professor John Keating in *Dead Poet's Society*?

The way we view our relationships to students and other faculty will shape our approach to lessons, one-on-one meetings, and individual work. It will influence how we assess our success and our failures and the roles we take on as educators. For example, in the film *Kindergarten Cop*, starring Arnold Schwarzenegger, Detective John Kimble is a hardened officer on a mission to nab his archnemesis, Cullen Crisp, once and for all. To do it, the gruff detective has to go undercover in the role of a kindergarten teacher in order to suss out Crisp's former girlfriend, who has been in hiding for years.

At first, Kimble's internal metaphor is that of an authoritarian homicide detective. He expects his commands to be obeyed, and he anticipates handling a group of twenty five-year-olds will be snap because up to this point, everyone has respected Kimble's imposing and dominant nature. He even coerces an unwilling witness to testify against Crisp through sheer intimidation. But as anyone who has ever interacted with a kindergartener can tell you, five-year-olds respect nothing, and John Kimble is mowed down like a weed on his first day of teaching.

In order for the detective to be successful, he incorporates what he knows as a police officer into how he teaches and interacts with the children. He tells the students they are all enrolling in the police academy and he teaches them discipline and order within the confines of this paradigm. While you will hopefully not be trying to put drug dealers behind bars while working undercover, maybe you are interested in helping those in the justice system get their high school diploma or college degree as a step toward rehabilitation for a successful future post-incarceration. This is all up to you, but it's necessary to know where you are coming from as an educator, because it will shape every bit of the teacher you want to become.

Communication Theory

According to Merriam-Webster, communication is a process where information is exchanged between individuals through a common system of signs, symbols, or behaviors.[xxiv] From this definition alone, it is clear that educators cannot do their job successfully without good communication skills, as so much of what we do involves "exchanging information" with others.[xxv]

How would you be able to share what you know if you couldn't tell people about it, or draw a picture, or write down what you've learned? However, as simple and obvious as it might seem, there are numerous ways for communication to go awry. [xxvi] Perhaps there is a language barrier, or what one person considers to be obvious, another person does not. Let's consider a common communication activity. Imagine two people are working together to complete a simple task. Person A will give instructions and Person B will follow the directives. The task is to make a peanut butter and jelly sandwich.

Person A: Get out the bread, peanut butter, and jelly.

Person B: Get them out from where?

This is the very first directive and we've already encountered an issue. Person A assumed Person B would know where the needed items would be located and where to go to retrieve them. For all we know, Person B isn't even in the kitchen.

Person A: Set the food down on the counter and get out the bread.

Person B puts the peanut butter, jelly, and bread on the counter and removes all the bread from the bag. You see where this is going, don't you?

Person A: Take out just two pieces of bread and set them down on the counter. Now, twist the lid off the jar of peanut butter and spread it on one of the slices using a knife from the drawer on your left.

Here, you can see Person A has learned quickly, and has adopted more clear and precise directives to help Person B achieve the tasks needed to make our sandwich. But what happens if Person B doesn't know which of our three items is peanut butter and which one is jelly? Maybe Person B has watched all your other pupils make PB&J sandwiches so he knows what items are needed, but as a teacher you might be perplexed if he reaches for the jelly after you tell him to get the peanut butter.

We'll stop here with this task, but hopefully you can see some of the major flaws in this type of communication. One of the primary problems is that the information is flowing one way. Person B doesn't have the opportunity to ask clarifying questions like what flavor of jelly is preferred or which jar contains the peanut butter. When Person B can supply feedback, Person A can determine what instructions need to be more explicit. Are there barriers to communication, such as not being able to read the label of a jar; is it clear if Person B is even paying attention to the given directive? (xxvii) Below is an example of a two-way communication flow chart.

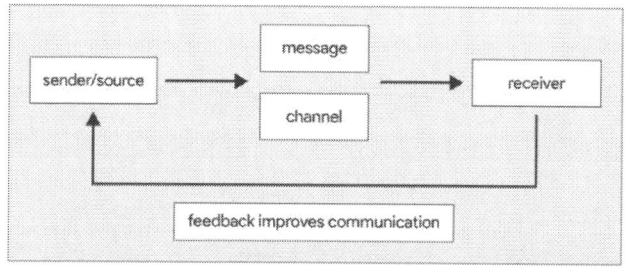

Figure 1: Two-Way Communication(xxviii)

Another very important thing to remember is that communication is far more than words, written or spoken. In the PB&J example above, Person B failed to use any kind of body language or other non-verbal communication to indicate what information might have caused confusion or concern. Person B could have pointed to the jars and shrugged his shoulders, indicating he didn't know which jar to choose to follow the instructions. In the famous words of Ursula, the Sea Witch, from Walt Disney's *The Little Mermaid*, "Don't underestimate the importance of body language."

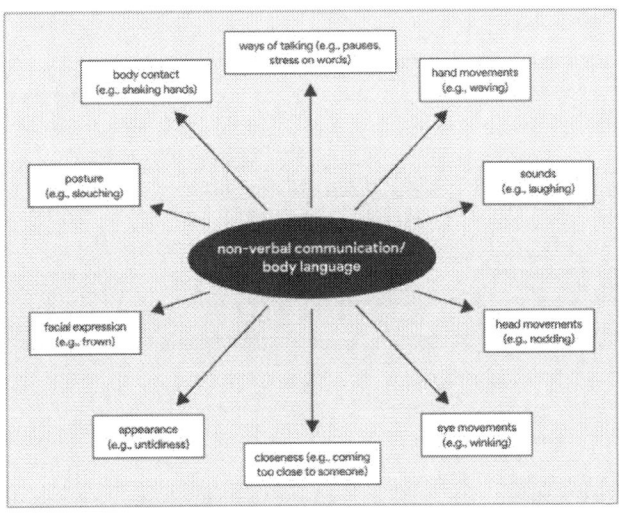

Figure 2: Non-Verbal Communication [xxix]

As an educator, you can use body language to see how you're coming across to your learners. [xxx] Students who are slumped over, glancing around the room, or fiddling with other things on their desk are often disinterested in what's going on around them. You can use these subtle clues to know if it's time for a break from learning so people can walk off some energy and come back and refocus. You'll also be able to figure out if your students are confused by the perplexed expressions on their faces, despite a lack of questions asking for clarification. You'll know you may need to back up and try another approach to the material. Non-verbal communication is just as powerful, if not more so, than words in text or speech.[xxxi]

It's also important to realize that how you communicate with your learners can and should include teaching aids. As we've said several times, different students learn differently, and as an educator, you need to be prepared to tackle that. For students who learn through visual cues, you can include typical visual aids such as slides and projected images, but you can also provide a demonstration.

Imagine taking a pottery class. The visual learner will watch how the teacher moves his hands over the clay, how much pressure is applied to the pedal of the potter's wheel to increase its speed, and how a skillful potter removes excess clay from the wheel to make beautiful designs. It is through seeing these actions that the student learns the process from the teacher.

Similar techniques will be used by those who need to learn by doing, either by working through concepts and problems to figure out solutions as they tackle a task, or through tactile response. If we consider the previously mentioned lesson of teaching fractions with the segments of a Hershey's Chocolate Bar, that is an excellent example of a tactile lesson. There are twelve equal pieces in every Hershey's Chocolate Bar. The teacher may ask, "How much of the candy bar would you like to eat? One twelfth of the chocolate bar or 11/12 of the chocolate bar?" By moving the pieces around and playing with the different configurations, a good communicator can show her students how different fractions make a whole.

Accepting Feedback

Through all of this, it's important to remember that people aren't born with the ability to communicate well. Good communication skills are learned and developed over time with practice, positive and critical feedback, and continually cycling though this ongoing process of evaluation, assessment, and improvement.[xxxii] Teachers in a school system, and even those who educate through organizational development for an employer, usually experience this cycle annually when employee evaluations are completed. Teachers in the public or private school setting likely receive it more often as they experience observations from students, other teachers, principals, superintendents, and even grade-level coaches.

But what if you're not a teacher in a traditional classroom setting? That doesn't mean assessment, feedback, and evaluation are any less

important to your growth and development as an educator. Are there people in your community you trust to give high-quality and accurate assessment? Think about joining a professional group, where mentor/mentee relationships play a role in the development of educators for your craft. Are there classes you can take to help improve your skills as a teacher, just as you have taken classes to boost your expertise as a hairstylist, for example?

Ask yourself, would you go to a hairstylist and trust that person to cut or color your hair if he or she hadn't attended any hair styling courses is five years? How about ten or twenty? It's the same idea if you aren't working on honing your craft as an educator. Figure three is an excellent model to get you started on asking for and accepting evaluation. Don't stop there. Evaluate what you did well after each time you teach and consider creating your own file of notes and observations, similar to the one that inspired this book, to document what you learned as you taught a challenging lesson and what you want to do differently next time.

About the style of presentation

- *Does the teacher speak clearly?*
  (loud enough; not too fast; faces the class; avoids mannerisms like 'um')

- *Is the teacher's non-verbal communication suitable?*
  (appropriate gestures and expressions; moves around; eye contact with whole class)

- *Does the teacher speak understandably?*
  (uses words that the students should be able to understand)

- *Is the speed of presentation right?*
  (the students must be able to absorb the material that is presented)

- *Is there two-way communication?*
  (the teacher checks regularly if the students have understood)

- *Is there evidence of a good relationship between teacher and students?*
  (teacher and students respect each other, listen to each other)

About the content

- *Does the teacher emphasise important knowledge?*
  (the main messages are clear and emphasised, unnecessary detail is left out)

- *Is information presented in a logical sequence?*
  (bits of information follow logically after each other - easy to understand and remember)

About the place where the teaching is happening

- *Is the place conducive to good communication?*
  (enough light; no noise from outside)

- *Are the students comfortable?*
  (adequate seating; students can see the teacher; not too hot/too cold)

About the use of teaching aids

- *Are the teaching aids relevant?*
  (the aids only deal with the subject matter of the lesson, and clarify it)

- *Are the teaching aids well prepared?*
  (only contain highlights/main points; neat; different colors are used)

- *Are the teaching aids easy to read and understand?*
  (letters and pictures are large enough; not too much crammed onto one aid)

- *Are the teaching aids skilfully used?*
  (the teacher handles them with confidence; uses a pointer; does not mix them up)

Figure 3: Communication and Evaluation Checklist[xxxiii]

Communicating with Others

When teaching, children in particular, communicating how much you care about your students can be crucial to their success. Children from pre-K through high school will be willing to connect to you if they know your concern for them is genuine. But learning how to communicate this can be a little tricky. The easiest and best way to do this is by getting to know your students. Learn what they like, what they're afraid of, what their biggest hopes and dreams are. Then do what you can to support them. Those students will never forget your honesty, and thoughtfulness. I know this as deeply as I knew as a fifth-grade student in Mrs. Stegall's class that she really did love me as her student. While the small things you do may not seem like much to you, sometimes they mean the world to a child.

Often when we educate young people, they come as a package deal with parents and siblings. Educating a child with a robust and positive support network is a joy to behold because that child has the tools of success at her fingertips. Sometimes, however, we have to share some difficult or less than pleasant news about those we teach with parents or other caregivers. It's important for teachers to show how much they care while also balancing what they say with tact and professionalism.

I made an observation recently about two participants in a Facebook group geared toward moms. In this particular post, the mother, Rachel, was looking to assess her gut reaction to an interaction she'd had with a teacher earlier that day and wanted feedback from other parents.

Essentially, Rachel's son had received detention, but because she was alerted via automated phone call, Rachel didn't know what her son had done to warrant that action. Unsurprisingly, Rachel's son was not forthcoming, only mentioning that the incident involved his art teacher.

Rachel decided to call her son's teacher to find out what had happened so she could confront her son about his behavior in school. When Rachel recounted the conversation with the teacher, she stated that the art teacher had informed her that her son had been goofing around at the beginning of class, attempting to sit at a table with his friends when the child was aware that current COVID-19 social distancing policies did not permit that. The teacher further explained that the child had been passing notes back and forth with these other students, and when the teacher confiscated the notes they contained inappropriate content. And finally, the teacher stated that the boys in this group of friends had been slow to pack up at the end of class. She had offered to not say anything about the inappropriate notes if the boys finished packing up and left the class quickly, as the teacher stated she didn't get paid to work at the school after 2:30 p.m. The teacher also mentioned that she had planned to send Rachel an email about all of this, but she simply forgot to hit the send button on the email after she typed it.

Rachel was livid when she hung up the phone. Her post in the mom's group labeled the art teacher unprofessional, a blackmailer, and unstable. All that from one single phone call, but if you were Rachel, would you feel the same? While the teacher has some gripes, her choice of tone and language didn't communicate caring, understanding, or even the slightest devotion to teaching. Instead, it showed that she was bothered by enforcing rules that ensured the safety of her students, willing to overlook concerning conduct in order to hasten her own ability to leave (she doesn't get paid to be at work after 2:30 p.m., remember), and while Rachel referred to the teacher as "unstable," further elaboration on this comment clarified that "ditzy" might have been a better choice of words. One descriptor Rachel definitely got right, however, is that the art teacher was completely unprofessional.

Activity – Rachel's Redo: Imagine you are Rachel, and you've just received an automated phone call stating your son needs to complete a detention in the next five school days. After speaking with your son, you decide to call his art teacher to find out what happened in class today that caused your son to earn a detention. What would you want to hear about the incident outlined above that might make you feel as if you and your child's teacher were on the same team as educators and parents?

Now let's switch roles. Imagine that you are the art teacher who is getting the phone call from Rachel. Using the questions below, come up with a better case presentation than the actual art teacher did. Keep in mind, your goal is to objectively present the situation while showing that you care about your students.

- Consider telling Rachel something about her son that makes you enjoy having him in your class.

- How might you rephrase some of the "gripes" the art teacher referenced above?

- How can you stress the importance of ushering students to follow dismissal procedures without making it sound like the students you serve in your position are a burden to be coped with until the clock strikes half past two?

- What do you do about the notes with inappropriate content? Do you tell Rachel about them, keep that information to yourself, or mention the notes but state you handled the issue in class (if you actually did so)?

- How might you finish up your phone call with Rachel to reaffirm her confidence you have her child's best interest at heart and want him to succeed and enjoy being in school, but to do so safely and respectfully?

- Do you think you handled this difficult situation well as an educator, and what might you do in the future? Do you think you adequately voiced your concerns to the parents while maintaining tact and professionalism?

Remember, you are not a lone ranger. While teaching can and often does take place in a classroom where you are the sole adult in a sea of many children, good schools and educator networks don't abandon you to figure everything out for yourself. Teaching can and should be a collaborative effort. Many teachers and educators teach in teams or collectives to design complimentary lessons. [xxxiv] Teachers are often faced with coping through or helping students handle some of life's most difficult experiences, and it's important to have support from others who know what you experience and can provide feedback. [xxxv] Seeking out the advice and communion of other educators will serve to enhance your skills as a listener and problem solver.

Now that you have the building blocks to be a good communicator, how do you put those pieces together to become a master of exposition? If you freeze up or get tongue-tied every time you stand up in front of the class, you may start to wonder if you have what it takes to be a teacher. Don't worry, this sensation is completely normal, as are the concerns of how you will ever teach a class if you stumble and fall all over your words. This is exactly what we will cover in the next chapter.

Chapter 4: How to Explain Content Well

One of the main duties of teachers is to explain things; they need to present new information in a way students will understand. If you are an educator, explanation just became one of your primary tasks, as well. Giving directions, describing subject matter, talking about theories and concepts that guide us are just a few among the many tasks explanation involves.

But what does it mean to "explain"? By definition, to explain is to make known, to make something understandable, or to show a logical progression of a relationship. [xxxvi] The goal of an explanation is to describe or communicate in a way that brings about clarity and understanding. However, this can be quite the challenge as not everyone learns in the same way. Explanation is really the examination of different ways of interpreting or viewing. What do I mean by this?

Let's look at chocolate chip cookies. I can *describe* what chocolate chip cookies are. When I tell you they are sweet treats made of sugar, flour, butter, eggs, and spices mixed with chunks of chocolate and baked in the oven until they reach the desired consistency for chewy or crunchy cookies, you can begin to get an idea of what they might taste or look like. I could get out a sketch pad and draw some cookies on a plate to *illustrate* to you what chocolate chip cookies look like. You will know what they are when you see them. My personal favorite would be to *make* them for you, so when they have baked up nicely we can share a delicious snack together and you will be able to recognize the cookies by their taste. All of the above are explanations of chocolate chip cookies meant to help you identify and understand what makes them unique from the hundreds of other cookies that exist.

When thinking about explanation, think about a scientist taking a deep dive into any particular topic. Scientists use experimentation, analysis, collaboration, and peer-reviewed research as they ask questions to get to the bottom of what they are trying to understand or learn about. We call this the scientific method. This method is important to remember when you explain concepts to your students.

As you are describing material, concepts, facts, and knowledge, try out differing methods to present information. Don't rely on one style of learning day in and day out. Remember that some students need to practice the concepts to fully comprehend them. What do I mean here?

- One day present the material as you regularly would; you talk, the students listen.

- The next day, at the beginning of your class ask them to grab a pen and paper and write down whatever they remember about yesterday's material. You can also ask specific questions here. (The idea of a quick test can make some students anxious. Make sure to assure them that this is a knowledge retention survey and not a deliberate move to ruin their grades.)

- The next day, organize your students to work in groups. Give each group an aspect of the material and instruct them about how they should present it to the rest of the class. My personal favorite practice in this setting is interactive presentation. Students tend to zone out when their peers are holding a presentation. But if they expect to be called out at any moment, they will be more likely to follow, and therefore learn.

Finally, don't forget about body language when you explain. As an instructor, analyze the facial expressions of those you teach to ensure they are grasping the knowledge you're sharing. The look of confidence should be returned to you as ideas and fundamentals take root and become synthesized as knowledge.

Communication Skills for Effective Explanation [xxxvii]

Before we get into the ins and outs of explanation, we should review some of the basics of communication related to explaining. Below, I go over some points to take into account when educating others.

<u>Be Respectful</u>: One of the most important things for an educator to know is that you, too, must be respectful of those you teach. This means using an appropriate tone and choice of words. If you're in a classroom this could be different depending on the age you teach. A teacher in an elementary classroom would generally have a different cadence and tone than a high school teacher, and this changes yet again when working with adult learners in a training or community learning atmosphere. Remember to give the speaker your attention by looking them in the eye and not interrupting or speaking over them. When you model how to speak and listen respectfully, your students will see its value.

<u>Repeat Your Lesson in Different Ways</u>: Keep in mind that some people may not understand what you are saying or what objective you are teaching the first time around. But they may not dare or bother to express that they didn't get it.

Therefore, it's not only important for you to repeat what you are trying to teach in several different ways, but to also consider how to present the multiple styles of learning as we've previously discussed for visual and tactile learners.

Check for Understanding: This one can be a bit trickier because you really have to test the learner's knowledge in some way. It's not enough to simply ask if they understand the lesson, as most students will respond affirmatively or not all. By asking students to summarize the lesson in one sentence or answer multiple-choice questions, you can see how much students understood from the lesson and where you may need to go back and address some areas where students are struggling.

Pay Attention to Body Language: It's important to pay attention to both your body language and that of your pupils. If you have a student who is confused and seems to be lost as you are covering the material, it's a sign that this student may need some individual attention for this lesson. Try pairing this student up with a stronger partner for group work. Your body language is also telltale. If every time a certain student speaks you roll your eyes or cross your arms, furrow your brow, and glare at her in anger, that student will never trust you enough to see you as an ally in her education. Think about body language as a two-way communication mode, just the same as any verbal communication exchange.

Think back to the beloved children's story, *Miss Nelson Is Missing.* Miss Nelson and Miss Swamp are the same person, but one version of the teacher the children loved, though she was probably too lax with classroom management to be an effective educator. The other version was despised so much that when faced with the possibility of being taught by Miss Swamp for the rest of the year, the children became despondent and their spirits were broken. It's not easy to find the happy middle ground, but it's important that you remember and utilize the information above in an effort to not approach your job in either a lackadaisical or overbearing manner.

Skills for Effective Explanation

Albert Einstein said if you can't explain something simply, you don't understand it well enough. (xxxviii, xxxix)

I agree with Einstein: if one can't simplify a concept well enough to present it to a ten-year-old, they may need to learn some more about the topic. Even ideas from astrophysics can be conveyed in an easy-to-follow manner. When such explanations won't capture is depth. And to be fair, often that's beyond the point of a conversation. But when it comes to transferring new material to a student, explaining well isn't the end goal but rather the first step. When we teach human anatomy in biology class, for instance, it's not hard to present the heart's main function in a simple way. Our heart pumps our blood and thus it keeps us alive. If the heart stops, we die. This is a good starting point but it lacks depth, complexity, and context. Where is the blood coming from? Where does it go when the heart pumps it out? Why do we die if the blood stops circulating in our body? How do we die? What can be done to mitigate the risk of a heart failure?

An easy-to-grasp idea is good if it awakens curiosity for more knowledge. A good explanation is tied to sound, well-thought-out strategies and lesson planning when it comes to teaching others. You must know what the levels of knowledge are you want to transfer and then know how, when, and why to do it. If you try to approach teaching without solid lesson planning for either child or adult learners, you are going to be in a world of hurt—what is referred to as "up a creek without a paddle."

It's easy to think that you know a certain subject backwards and forwards and therefore lesson planning is unnecessary. Wrong! Stand up in front of any group, no matter how large or how small, no matter what age, tripping over your words in a lack of preparation, and you will see that having a plan is imperative. This is actually a very common error teachers make; they forget how it feels to not know or not understand a subject. It takes some amount of humbleness and care to remember, whatever feels obvious to you doesn't feel the same way to your students—even if you're teaching adults. In this section, we will discuss some ideas that will be useful for considering lesson strategies.

<u>Storytelling</u>:[xl] Storytelling is a great tool for communicating data and information. It's one I often use in the books I write. Not only does it provide connection for the reader, but also, more importantly, it provides context and meaning. Qualitative research is often referred to as storytelling, sometimes derisively, but its main purpose is to address the deeper meaning of the study. Human beings evolutionarily connect better to stories as they are emotionally engaging, leave room for imagination, and they build rapport.

For example, the divorce rate is higher between couples who did not graduate high school. A qualitative study would interview participants to find that perhaps on average, over a five-year span, these couples experienced five job changes and two bouts of unemployment. This had such a financial strain on the marriage that the couples could not overcome irreparable harm and dissolved the marriage. This is not the type of information that a quantitative study would find. Putting what you want your students to learn into a story can help them remember and understand the data and concepts.

Be Concise:[xli] Michael Pollan, a writer who covers a wide variety of content from psychedelics to nutrition, wrote a 450-page book on food. It was quite a tome, and the book was extremely detailed and much more than what your average foodie would be looking to read. Several years later he rewrote the book, cutting it down to 250 pages, but it was still too in-depth for what the average reader was looking for. The third installment of the book, *Food Rules,* was released to include 64 directives distilled from the initial 450 pages. They are basic food-related advice such as "if your grandma doesn't recognize it as food, don't eat it." This book became a *New York Times* Bestseller.

When you think about explaining a concept, break it down to its most basic properties and build from there. Don't try to explain the full principle in its entirety, as it may be too confusing for those who are unfamiliar with what you are teaching. This is called scaffolding. It's impractical to think you can explain every aspect of a topic at once, as it takes time for students to learn and synthesize knowledge. [xlii] Heed Einstein's words.

Reciprocal Teaching: [xliii] As we addressed briefly in the previous section, body language can be an indicator of which students are struggling and lead you to pair stronger students in group work with them. When the stronger student explains concepts to struggling students, this is called reciprocal teaching. When this happens, the student who was high performing will help others though an almost Q&A type system, though it doesn't have to involve direct questions.

Through clarification and explanation, the high-performing students benefit from the power of repetition. They also adopt new skills such as teaching. And surely, they will help to increase the knowledge of the students they assist.

Make a Connection to the Real World:[xliv] Some learners struggle with abstract concepts because they can't visualize or experiment with them in the classroom. As an educator, it's still your job to ensure these individual students end up understanding what is in the curriculum. The other day, I was looking through a stack of nuclear engineering thesis titles, and let me assure you there were words that meant nothing to me. They might as well have been in another language. High Entropy Alloy—What is that? What is the Two-Fluid Model? Just because I am a former engineer doesn't mean I understand all the concepts and principles of engineering in their entirety. I need them to be connected to what I know for the concepts to make sense.

While you won't always be able to make these individual connections in a classroom, look for other materials, like videos or walkthroughs, that can help show students how the abstract relates to things they may experience for real. A concrete example can help solidify an understanding that may have not been possible before.

More than anything, it's important to understand that simply explaining something clearly, or what you may perceive as clearly, isn't enough. You have to take into account that learners come to you at different levels in an educational range. Just because students in a particular grade level are "supposed" to know something does not mean they do. Teaching cooking for beginners at your community class, you may have someone who has never so much as cooked scrambled eggs, and someone else who is there to improve their ability to put together meals and everything in between. What is important is that you need to be able to work with all of these students to enable them to acquire knowledge. So how do you do that? Active learning.

98

Chapter 5: Active Learning

When my son, David, was in tenth grade he went on a field trip to an amusement park with his science class. The purpose of the field trip was that as the students rode the fun adventure rides, they would collect specific measurements to calculate velocity, force, and whatever else was requested from the teacher. However, in David's case, the teacher left all the worksheets back at the school and didn't realize this until they had already made it to the amusement park, meaning the kids simply got a free play day at Six Flags.

Had the day gone off the way it was supposed to, he would have had a day of active learning, which is when students engage in learning through doing. It is a contrast to passive types of knowledge acquisition such as listening to lectures or watching presentations. Here, we see the focus change from what the teacher is doing to what the student is doing. We are particularly looking for the student to have a high level of engagement in the learning process. This is why the semester I had the syllabus with errors had gone off so poorly. Because fewer and fewer students came to class, there was less and less active learning going on.

I used to teach many discussion-based courses. Along with lecture-based teaching, these are the two most common teaching styles most educators utilize, but they don't fit every scenario. Discussion would never work in the large lecture section of a Biology 101 course on a large college campus, and lecture is completely out of place in the smaller corporate training atmosphere. As the educator, you have to examine who your audience is, what you're trying to achieve, and why you're educating the group in the first place. This way you can make the decision as to what method works best and when. It could be that you use a mix of both methods. Do you have a preference of methodologies and if so, why?

Preconditions for Active Learning [xlv]

Just like all other types of lesson planning, active learning also takes *preparation*. This means knowing who your students are and how they behave. If you're pairing students up, putting together those who cut up or make mischief isn't a good idea. Let well-performing students lead students who struggle in some reciprocal teaching. It is a wonderful way to help build mastery and understanding. But you need to know who these students are. Learners should have a syllabus, so they know when this kind of active learning experience is coming. If this is a one-time interaction, go over what your learner should expect from the experience. This way they will know if they are on track or not and can fill in their knowledge gaps with additional home study. Performing in front of their peers is a serious deal, especially for younger students. Knowing how to prepare in advance will help soothe their anxiety so they can pay attention to instructions rather than worry if they have done something "wrong." Additionally, ensure you've prepared all your written instructions and have assigned any out-of-class work to be completed before the active learning experience.

Techniques to Promote Active Learning [xlvi]

Group Activities

Case-based learning is when learners use the knowledge they have to approach how they would handle a real-world situation. This type of activity is used a lot in law and medical schools, but it can be applicable in any type of learning environment. Simply provide a scenario or vignette for the student/s to address areas they know have relevance, any other information they might need to make decisions about the case, and what the long-term implications may be of any decision they made. This is a really effective active learning practice for small groups.

Another option is *Group Discussion*. The questions groups are asked to consider should be thought provoking enough to inspire deep thinking or even a friendly debate. You don't want students to come to an immediate conclusion. The goal of this type of group discussion is for students to consider how the material they learned impacts the question and come to a conclusion based on it.

You can organize *Group Teaching* as a form of group activity. Each group is assigned a principle or concept to explain and teach to the rest of the class. After the appropriate amount of time for preparation, each group should teach the concept they received to the rest of the class. As I mentioned before, interactive presentation should be encouraged as it keeps everyone more present and attentive.

Individual Activities

One activity that works well for individuals rather than groups is *Application Cards.* Here, after you have taught a principle, concept, or theory, distribute index cards to the students and ask them to provide a real-world example of what they have just learned.

Ask students to *Directly Paraphrase* a lesson or part of a lesson. You can make this activity harder by providing more restrictions, such as asking for the paraphrasing to be for a specific purpose.

Ask students to write a *One-Minute Paper* that focuses on the learning objective of the lesson.

Encourage them to think critically about it. After one minute, tell everyone to share what they wrote to stimulate discussion in the class.

The flip side of this practice is asking students to think about their *Muddiest Point* of the lecture. What areas have them confused? Why? Motivate them to give feedback about it. This practice can give you real insight about what parts of the lecture you may need to reteach, explain differently, or address more in depth.

And finally, challenge your students to give a *One-Sentence Summary* on the overall concepts of the material using the format What? How? or Why?

Partner Activities

Have students *Role Play* a part as an active learning experience. This could be used in a variety of settings. Appoint a young child in your class to be Abraham Lincoln as he reads out part of the Emancipation Proclamation. Doctors regularly use role playing as they simulate patient scenarios to help them figure out a diagnosis, but also learn how to interact with patients. Tell your students to demonstrate how they would respond in any given situation.

Assign each student a partner for *Think-Pair-Share* discussion. Ask them a question that requires a higher level of thinking skills. You can refer to the application, analysis, or evaluation levels of Bloom's taxonomy. Let's imagine you ask a student something like, "Should terminally ill patients have the right to decide when or if they want to die before the terminal disease takes their life?" Give the student a few minutes to write a response, pair him or her up with another student and give them about double the time to discuss their responses among one another. Let them share their responses with others in the class.

There is a faster version of think-pair-share called *Turn-and-Talk.* In this version you simply ask the pairs to talk together for a few moments before sharing their thoughts with the class.

The final partners' approach I'll discuss here is the *Devil's Advocate Approach.* [xlvii] This activity assigns one or more students to the opposite side of the prevailing argument. This is more or less a classic debate approach where you allow a free communication flow between your students. You can help them with auxiliary questions if you feel they need it. You should also step in to chill the mood if the argument becomes heated. I would encourage you to take notes about interesting, smart, thought-provoking, or absolutely incorrect points students bring up. Once the debate is over, go through your notes and ask your students why they said what they said, why do they think that and so on. If they said something that's incorrect or even offensive, without pointing fingers or public humiliation, ask questions from that student until they realize why their words were inaccurate. Avoid phrases such as, "You were wrong," or, "That's a mean thing to say." Rather package the message into questions: "So now that we had this discussion, do you still think that...?" or, "If someone said that about you, how would you feel?" Avoid direct blame, help the students with their mistake and make them say the words "I was wrong." This way they will learn a much deeper and better lesson.

Visual Organizing Activities

Ask students to complete a *Categorizing Grid* by providing them with a grid of categories and list or bank of jumbled words, pictures, or math problems to sort these into their proper category.

Have students draw out a *Concept Map*, which is used to show the relationship between different ideas. These maps are represented by having a key notion in the center and then others around it with labeled arrows describing the relationship. You can ask students to complete this activity for any lesson where an idea is influenced by a relational concept.

Ask students to categorize concepts based on whether specific *defining features are or are not present.*

Provide students with *demonstrations* in the classroom. Ask the student to predict what will happen prior to your *demonstration*. Afterward, pair students into groups to discuss how their prediction may or may not have differed from what actually occurred and why.

Have students create a *memory matrix. Memory matrices* are tables created to be filled in as the student learns more about the topic at hand. For example, if we wanted students in a nutrition class to learn more about how sugar and sugar substitutes impact the different systems of the body, we might have a table that looks like this:

Sugar/ Sugar Substitute	Circulatory/ Cardiovascular	Gastric/ Digestive	Endocrine	Renal
Glucose				
Sucralose				
Aspartame				
Saccharin				
Stevia				

As students learn more about how sugar and sugar substitutes affect these different systems, they fill in the matrix. With the help of this exercise, we take what is learned through didactic methods and reinforce the information through active learning.

Similar to the *defining feature grid,* students could also create a *pros and cons list* as they pertain to the topic at hand.

A somewhat fun experiment is giving students the strips of a shredded piece of paper and asking them to reassemble the paper. Depending on the size of the shredded piece and how distinct the page is, this can be a maddening activity. It can also tell you a lot about students and their motivations. Some are determined to never leave a task incomplete, while others are immediately put off by the sheer amount of energy they need to put into simply flipping all the pieces of paper over to the same side.

Visual modeling or mini maps are like *concept maps,* but with a much smaller list of terms. Students should use them to create a logical structure between them, as well as using arrows to show relationships. Encourage students to share and answer any questions others have about their maps.

By now we've worked with students who are passive learners and those who are active learners. We've approached learning from various angles to test that we have gotten our message through to as many of our learners as possible. Our next task is to make sure that what we teach sticks. So much of what is learned can be here today and gone tomorrow. My goal in the next chapter will be to show you how turn the information you teach into permanent knowledge.

Chapter 6: Knowledge Application for Lasting Learning

When I was in college I took an English class on Romantic Literature. It was one of the absolute most horrific courses I ever attended for a number of reasons. One of them was the amount of sheer memorization the professor expected. I was fully capable of reading a text, processing and analyzing it, and drawing conclusions in relation to other texts based on what I'd read. This professor would simply slap text on the exams verbatim and want us to list the author and title of the work. I hadn't prepared for that because this was a class in my senior year, and I assumed that level of knowledge to be egregiously low.

For the final exam in the course I studied hard, but there was really too much to memorize: Byron, Shelley, Blake, and so much more. As I was finishing going through Samuel Taylor Coleridge's *Kubla Kahn* one more time, it hit me that I really should tell the professor I had memorized all the poems and literature. But a Person from Porlock—a term that has come to symbolize "interrupted genius" after Coleridge claimed to have been interrupted by such a person in the middle of writing *Kubla Kahn*—had interrupted me, and therefore I should just get an A on the exam for the effort and be done. I was not the only student with this idea. The moral of this story: cramming is a notoriously poor method of teaching and learning.

To ensure students retain what they learned beyond the unit, the final exam, and the state exam, is actually a big challenge for teachers. Knowledge is foundational and we continuously build on it. Learners will always need a strong and solid educational foundation to have a strong, solid, and successful future. Those students with a cracked foundation, even if it is in only one topic or area, will struggle through school.

When David was a boy his mother had the hardest time getting him to learn his multiplication tables. When he started division, David continued to wrestle with the treacherous numbers. Finally, one night she sat him down at the dinner table. She told David that multiplication and division worked the same. And if he would sit down and learn to multiply, he would automatically learn simple division. This would then serve him when he got to long division in a few weeks. If he didn't do it, he was going to have a harder time as his lessons became more complex. David worked hard and learned to multiply, and his mother simultaneously explained how the same numbers worked for simple division to bring him up to speed. David's math classes got easier for him and he was able to follow along thanks to the well-laid foundation he received.

When students leave our classroom, training room, or even our dinner table, we want the knowledge we have imparted to be there for the long haul. There are a few things we can do to make sure what we teach sticks with our learners and doesn't disappear the moment they've left our presence.

Strategies to Encourage Lasting Learning

Group Work: Research has shown us time and time again that students retain more knowledge when they work in groups. Students who cooperate with others get more practice explaining things, expressing what they've learned, and describing their thought process and reasoning to others. This is not something students who work exclusively as an individual get the opportunity to engage in. It can make a big difference in the level of understanding the learner develops.

If you've ever asked students to pair off or get into groups and heard a collective groan, you might know that students sometimes resent working together. There are many reasons for this. Sometimes certain students carry more of the "academic" weight of the group while other group members do nothing. Others don't like that they cannot choose their own partners, and some students just prefer solitary work. It is for these reasons that we need to make sure we explain to students the purpose of group work.

You don't need to explain that in Group A you want Kyle to become a reciprocal teacher and gain mastery while leading the group. That could be awkward for everyone involved. However, you can easily tell your learners that they will get more from the training or class if they are able to express their reasoning and hear others' reasoning as well. They can discuss the material and make educated decisions with others who have a different perception than themselves.

Writing: When students enter kindergarten, one of the first things they learn to do is write. For the rest of their lives, they will use writing as a mechanism for learning. The same is true of reading. Both reading and writing have become reciprocal in the educational process. Today we use technology to meet both of these ends. If I want to know something, I get online. I have to be able to evaluate good and bad sources of information, but everything I need is there for me on the Internet in articles and videos. By the same token, writing is a way for individuals to explore thinking. Some people examine their thoughts and feelings through keeping a personal journal, while others have a creative process and write novels or poetry as a means of emotional expression. And still other people, like myself, write to express ideas about thinking, learning, and teaching.

Writing has the ability to enhance memory and, though I am not writing for a creative process, it stimulates my imagination. When I write outlines for these books, I don't plan to cover all the stories or tales about my life I end up sharing, but as I am writing my memory is jogged and the example that fits with what I am trying to express comes to mind. I have triple-checked my work to make sure I haven't said anything too embarrassing or that would mortify my wife— and all that checking cements my own knowledge as well.

Encourage students to develop some form of daily writing or notetaking practice, preferably in a composition notebook, or a traditional journal. When they engage multiple senses into note taking, that mere fact deepens learning.[xlviii] They don't have to fill pages; a paragraph or two will do the magic. Writing helps students to think about what they know and to wander into the realm of what they might *want* to know. Additionally, developing a personalized writing style and voice is never a bad idea.

Evaluating Information: We are bombarded with information twenty-four hours per day, seven days a week, 365 days a year. The information flow passing over the average first-world citizen is constant—unless they make a conscious decision to unplug. That choice comes with a host of consequence, like everyone wanting to know why they were "missing" and an endless number of text and voice mail messages to return to. Considering this constant informational input, it is imperative you teach your students what is and is not a reliable source of information. Students need to know what biases are and that everyone is subject to them. As educators we need to help our students learn to validate information, and show them the impact of what can happen when inaccurate information is considered to be true.

We need to ensure our students know the value of remaining reasonably skeptical as they consider whether or not a piece of information is accurate. Let students know that scholarly sources from peer-reviewed journals are the ultimate quality of information they need to look for. If the results of a study can be repeated, that's a bonus.

In comparison, articles published by websites like *The Onion* are not reliable because *The Onion* is a digital media company that produces satire. Their articles should not be viewed as truthful, but instead through a lens of ridicule and scorn. However, in 2018, State Representative of Tennessee, Micah Van Huss cited *The Onion* when making a legitimate argument regarding a bill in the Tennessee General Assembly floor having to do with freshmen basketball players mercilessly hazing seniors. The satirical article offered that this "hazing" was the reason why the basketball coach at the University of Kentucky, John Calipari, was benching all the freshmen players and only let seniors play. [xlix]

Experiential Learning:[l] As we discussed earlier in this book, experiential learning is just what it sounds like: learning through personal experience. However, most of the learning conservation occurs via reflection. In order to have something to reflect on, students must have worthwhile educational experiences such as internships, co-ops, shadowing opportunities, or a coursework experience that is appropriately challenging. According to Dr. Todd Cherches at New York University, experiential learning can include multiple kinds of student engagement, some of which we have reviewed like discussion, knowledge-sharing, collaboration, connectivity, creativity, and synthesis. Some other options to consider include decision-making, risk-taking, and analysis. As an instructor you have many opportunities to include positive and worthwhile educational experiences in your classes and ask your students to reflect on them.

Let's think about experiential learning through the context of cooking. While we are going to provide an experiential process to teach this topic, as educators, we have to appreciate our students as individuals and realize they may approach this task differently. You could have students who prefers to learn by watching you make the dish, observing you add ingredients and cook them up before venturing out on their own. Another learner might come in with her favorite book of recipes and cooking techniques, already having ideas in her mind about how she would prepare different types of dishes. And yet another student might come to class ready to jump into cooking with no instruction whatsoever, reading the instructions line by line as they go.

The Five Rs:[li] Recall, Rehearse, Review, Reflect, and Refine—these are the five Rs and they are meant to help learners retain information over time. Information that has to be learned and synthesized, absorbed, and analyzed is easier to remember because deep learning takes place as part of those processes. However, there are times when learners benefit from rote memorization. The five Rs can help anchor this kind of learning process.

You can begin by having students *recall* the data they need to have learned. There are numerous ways to do this; pop quizzes, fun games, on the spot, rapid-fire questions. The goal of recalling is to gather information about which areas of the material are not well-memorized or understood by your students. They need extra work on those parts.

In the time leading up to a test, have your students *rehearse* the material they've been working on. Offer a mock exam before an upcoming assessment. This can be especially helpful in the K-12 school system, where there is a large push for children to perform well on standardized state testing. Because so much is riding on the scores of these tests, it can be a good idea to offer a mock test in the fall, not only to provide children an opportunity to understand what will be expected of them, but also to provide educators with a baseline of learning. While these tests should not be held against the children in any way, they can be used as indicators, along with other factors, as to which children may be behind peers and need after-school tutorials. Those who may have learning disabilities and should be referred for assessment can get special help too. Finally, teachers can see in which subjects the school is doing a great job.

The rehearsal also can let you know where you need to *review*. I believe it's important to remember the big picture and help our students remember it too. During the time of year that testing becomes prevalent, we place a lot of pressure on young minds to perform in a specific way. We need to work consistently with our learners and make sure they understand the purpose of what they are being taught. We then can help them retain information with specific schemas.

A schema is a method of cognitive structuring that helps us understand how things work. Schemas determine how we organize knowledge. When we learn new information, we connect it to existing knowledge, belief, or experience. Those connections create a type of structure in our brain.

These structures, or schemas, will help students quickly locate information at a later time when it is needed. By reviewing information with students, we are reinforcing these schemas to ensure information is correct and properly stored, waiting to be accessed for tests and assessments.

The ultimate goal is to *reflect* on the knowledge the student has and to help him or her further *refine* that knowledge. The 5Rs help students achieve mastery of the material. If conducted well, they will have a full grasp on the concepts and principles of any given topic. All students can reach this level, but not all students can reach it in the same amount of time or with the same type of resources.

Educational Apps for Learners

Today many of us live and die by technology. This is an obvious fact for those who are in the educational system today. As I was preparing to write this book, I researched a variety of classroom and learning methods for all ages. One of the scenes that struck me as both funny and telling was observing one of the first computer lab lessons for a group of young kindergarten students in a charter school. Many of these children did not know how to use a computer mouse, as they had used the touchscreen of a phone or tablet their entire lives. If they had used a mouse, it had been a touchpad on a laptop. Two frantic teachers trying to show twenty five-year-olds how to use a traditional mouse made me chuckle, but also pointed out how fast technology evolves. In response to that, I made a list of educational apps for tablets and phones students can enjoy:

Kahoot

Anki

Quizlet

Google Classroom, Remind, Class Dojo—Check and see if your child's teacher has a classroom set up.

Duolingo

Khan Academy

EdX—For High School and University Students

PhotoMath

SoloLearn

Epic

Hungry Caterpillar Play School

Khan Academy Kids

Goodness Shapes

Udemy

Quickmath Jr.

There is something here for every level, every subject, and every person. Many of these apps are free. Some of those geared toward younger children do not contain third-party advertisements. [lii]

In our next chapter, it will be time to delve into how to give constructive feedback. Being a teacher comes with a lot of unique power, sometimes power you don't even realize you have. Giving feedback and being aware of *how* you go about it can mean the difference between effective encouragement and crushing the learning spirit.

Chapter 7: Giving Constructive Feedback

In the small European village where I'm from, I was good friends with a boy a few years older than me. His name was Tomasz, and he was a gifted artist. His parents owned a farm, but they saved up their money, and when Tomasz graduated from our local school, his parents sent him to art school in the city. Tomasz came home around the holidays to help around the farm wherever he could, but mostly he talked about his art classes and how much he loved being in the city. He returned to school for the spring term, and I was happy for him. I thought he was on his way to becoming the artist he'd always dreamt of, that his paintings and sculptures would be shown in galleries one day.

One night in March of that year something happened. I had been out late on a date, and I saw the headlights on the old farm truck Tomasz's father drove bumping down the dirt road between our farms. I heard yelling because the windows on the truck were open. Tomasz was in the truck, shouting that he would never return to school. His father shouted back that he would because of what he and Tomasz's mother had sacrificed to nurture their son's talent.

The next morning, I went to visit my friend and find out why he'd returned home so abruptly and why he refused to go back. When I went down the hall to Tomasz's bedroom, I saw his bags open on the floor while he sat at his desk, looking over a painting with a note attached. I called out to my friend in greeting, but when he turned to face me, he ripped the painting in half and stormed past me, stating he had work to get to on the farm.

I walked into Tomasz's room and picked up the painting and note from the floor. The note was a harsh critique of my friend's work in red ink:

Tomasz, you've peaked! You call this art?
A child coloring could have done better.
There is no vision here, none at all.
Whatever potential you had is gone.

I was shocked by the content of that note. I remember it vividly even to this day. It was unbelievably harsh, and my friend, who was all of eighteen years old, took those words to heart. Tomasz did not produce art again for another thirty years, not until after the deaths of both of his parents. He felt he had let them down and was an utter disappointment to them, that he would never achieve his goals or the dreams his parents had for him.

The painting was beautiful to me, though I don't know much about art. Maybe it didn't meet the artistic level the instructor wanted, but that feedback committed an unforgiveable sin as far as I was concerned. This "teacher" had taken a raw talent and a passion to learn and snuffed them both out like they were nothing. Tomasz's story is a cautionary tale, and one I've always tried to keep in mind when working with others. This doesn't mean you don't tell others the hard truth about what they need to hear. It means you need to learn how to give feedback constructively, so students know what they do well and where they need to put in extra work. That is where we are going to spend our focus in this chapter.

How to Give Feedback (liii)

I think it goes without saying that Tomasz's art teacher did an extremely poor job at giving feedback. Perhaps that instructor had an off day, but if that's how he or she gave feedback on a regular basis, I cannot imagine how that person went on to have a successful career as an academic. If she was ripping students to shreds like she did to Tomasz, how many were likely to have stayed under her tutelage, and how many didn't fiercely return the favor during faculty evaluations? Was any of it even meant to improve performance anyway, or was it just some twisted form of academic bullying?

It's imperative to think about the feedback you need to give and how to give constructively. You won't always be able to say positive things about your students' work, their behavior, or their work ethic, but you can communicate effectively and with kindness.

Your feedback should have an *educational goal*. Let's consider the experience of Nina. She was a department chair in the English department and her specialty was creative writing, though she often taught a class here and there as needed in her department. Because she was so busy with administrative duties, she was highly selective about the doctoral students she accepted as advisees.

One day I was meeting her for lunch at the faculty club and she had a big smile on her face. When I asked her what she was so thrilled about, she replied she had just finished reading a short story by one of her students, and it was the most disgusting thing she'd ever read. Taken aback, I asked why she was so happy about that. It turns out she'd been working with the student for a while on finding his voice as author, and while the genre he preferred, gruesome and gore-filled horror, wasn't Nina's favorite, that student had finally found his author's voice.

Despite the fact Nina didn't personally like what this student wrote, she strived to help the aspiring Stephen King to improve his skill in order to benefit his craft. Her goal was always to boost the quality of what the student produced and not transform his work by forcing him into a box of what she found tasteful.

One way you can do what Nina did is to *ask questions.* What is possible for the student to achieve? What isn't possible? How can I help this student improve to reach the top of his or her personal abilities? If you want a student in math class today to subtract by borrowing from the tens column or add by carrying the two, you are going to have a major problem. Children don't learn math in that way anymore. The "new math" is what students learn. They not only don't know "old-school" math, but they also have to show their work using new methods. So if you're a parent to a kid who is learning online due to

COVID and you're fighting with your child over math because your child is confused about all this borrowing and carrying, you need to make sure to ask if your feedback is helping or hindering learning.

Teach students how to give peer-led feedback. Your opinions and thoughts aren't the only ones that matter. If you've done your job well, and I trust you have, then those you've educated have excellent minds fully capable of forming thoughts and opinions and providing constructive feedback too. Allow students to work in pairs or peer groups where they can share their work or explain how they reasoned their response. The goal here is to allow students to provide one another with differing points of view and perspectives, and help teach them the nature of giving constructive feedback as well.

Another strategy you can utilize is to the art of *good note making.* There are a number of different ways to implements this, such as utilizing sticky notes, like Post-Its, which can be good for providing individualized feedback that is both positive and critical. Instead of calling out Jack for his negative behavior, you can walk by his seat, casually placing a sticky note on his desk as a reminder not to shout out across the room. During my observations, I found this method particularly effective as a classroom management tool as teens didn't relish the idea of being called out and reprimanded in front of their peers. The teachers who used sticky notes to discipline also used them for applauding good behavior, so it was unclear what the note said and if it was congratulatory or not. However, students have reported that even writing feedback in a pen color other than red makes it easier to read and process it because they automatically associate red ink as negative and authoritarian.

More than anything, give those you educate *genuine praise*. No one is all bad. Educating is one of the hardest jobs in the world, and once parents were stuck at home, educating their children through the first phase of the COVID-19 pandemic, they began to realize just exactly how hard it really is. Some of that is because they aren't trained educators, and many of parents are juggling working from home at the same time their eight-year-old needs help in their Zoom class, and their three-year-old wants a snack. This pandemic has taught all of us that teaching is challenging position. I was pleased to see many parents acknowledging that for the first time. I didn't see quite so many Facebook grumbles about school supply lists this year.

I also hope many educators know that there is something positive to be said about every single person they educate. Yes, some students are frustrating and a pain in the butt, but they have positive qualities. You can find something nice to say about any learner. Perhaps that student who shows up to your chemistry class is loud and spastic because she's nervous, but she's always early and eager to learn and stays late to make sure the class is properly cleaned so you don't get stuck there doing all that heavy-duty work yourself. Maybe Lily in your fourth period English class has a bad attitude, but she writes beautiful poetry, and you can help her nurture that skill. Find something your student does well and praise them. You just might be the only person who has done so.

My wife was not brought up in a loving home, I'm sad to say. Her brother was often called stupid and "retarded," for lack of a better word, by her parents. He struggled in school and regularly brought home bad grades. He was told on a regular basis that he was too dumb to achieve anything in life and that he wouldn't amount to anything. When he was in high school, my wife's brother was tested for dyslexia and he was diagnosed with a learning disability. Instead of rallying around their son and helping him get the support he needed to finish his education, they responded by throwing their hands in the air and proclaiming that at least they now knew why he was so stupid.

When my wife told me this story about her brother, it reminded me so much of the cruelty Tomasz had endured as a young art student. I could not even imagine the pain of what it must feel like to receive that kind of criticism and verbal abuse from those who are at a minimum supposed to protect and love you. As educators, it's okay to get frustrated and overwhelmed, but bite your tongue and cap your pen. Don't say something you will live to regret. If there is no positive purpose to your words, there is no point in sharing them.

How to Improve Giving Feedback [liv]

<u>Don't Compare Learners</u>: Though it can be quite difficult, don't compare learners. It's simply not fair to them. Students should receive feedback based on their own progress and development. It's important to remember that learners exist on a spectrum; some will be at the top and some at the bottom and a whole bunch in between. If you are constantly comparing a student at the bottom of the spectrum to a student at the top, that student isn't likely to ever meet your expectations. But if you compare that student's progress and growth over time, you may find that he has increased his comprehension skills by 50 percent. Isn't that

something praiseworthy? Students are individuals, so make sure you treat them as such.

Be Specific: It's not enough to say "you did a great job" or "that was good." You need to be specific when you give feedback, whether positive or negative. If you're teaching a ballet class, you might say, "The way you performed your pirouettes in class today was excellent. Keep up the good work." Another example is, "Your plies weren't in proper form today. You need to practice them more." Those comments both provide specific feedback about what the student did or did not do well.

Give Specific Action: When you give feedback, you want to let others know how to move forward. In the example above, we tell our student to either "keep up the good work" or "practice more." Depending on what we teach, this could be any type of directive. Let's think of a few…

Take clear notes.

Keep a diary.

Work on your creative writing.

Practice differential equations.

Partner up and practice speaking only in French.

Each of these gives a direct action to help the learner improve in some way.

Don't focus on natural ability: While this advice seems counterintuitive, hear me out on it. Research has found that when educators give praise based on effort over smarts, students recognize that as intrinsic motivation. This creates a blueprint their brains will follow in the future. The type of feedback a learner receives shapes the kind of feedback they look to receive about themselves. The majority of students who receive praise for effort ask about how their peers perform in comparison to themselves, while those who do not receive this type of feedback generally ask about how they can improve their own performance. So focus on the process of learning, as it's more likely to feed a drive to yield results.

Improvement takes time. Provide your student with clear directives for what it takes to more forward toward their goals. Remember, some students will take baby steps while others will make leaps and bounds, and that's okay. If a student makes an error, help them back up and get back on track. Correct quickly, quietly, and with compassion. And don't forget to give your students high expectation and praise when it is earned.

All students are worthy of praise, and even the worst are not to be subject to cruelty. In our final chapter we are going to talk about working with difficult students. Some students are more challenging than others, and not all of us are prepared or have the resources to handle them.

Chapter 8: Coping with Difficult Students

In the past I attended some of my grandkids' kindergarten classes several days a week. I met other kids on their first day of school and would quietly observe them and the teachers periodically over the course of the fall term and into spring. One of the children I met right off the bat was named Lucas, and I could tell Lucas was different. He didn't seem to socialize much with the other children or know how to play with them. At recess he played by himself with the exception of throwing dirt at other children, and he was easily coaxed into fights. There was a small faction of boys in the class who knew how to push specific buttons that would cause Lucas to act out.

As the year continued, I noticed other things as I would stop by this classroom. One day I came to class and all the children had come to the carpet for circle time, but Lucas remained at his seat in the back of the room. His seat had also been moved. Most of the children were seated at the big half-moon table in the middle of the room, but Lucas was at a standalone desk that had been pushed up to one of the corners. Lucas's teacher mentioned he needed the extra space his desk provided and that he didn't like being close to others on the carpet. It usually led to hitting and kicking, and it was easiest to let Lucas decide if he wanted to come to the carpet or not.

One afternoon when Lucas came in from recess, he was in trouble because he'd thrown dirt at another child while playing and the two of them had gotten into an argument. Because one of the children involved had been having ongoing issues with Lucas most of the year, the teacher asked the principal to come get Lucas and speak to him about his behavior. It was beyond apparent Lucas was somewhere on the autism spectrum, but his parents had not requested any testing or services for him. So the teacher was trying to use the discipline process to encourage the parents to request services for their child, as this was one of the few resources she had.

When the principal came to retrieve Lucas and take him to his office, Lucas was undeniably scared and refused to go. He was worked up and had a meltdown in the hallway. He crawled under a desk that was used for a cooldown when students needed a break, and he screamed, kicking the walls. The principal, who was soft spoken, tried to calm the boy, but Lucas wasn't having it. At this point Lucas was totally disruptive. The kindergarten teacher returned to her class, leaving her assistant teacher, the assistant principal, and myself in the hallway. I was far down the hall, attempting to stay out the way.

The principal's next words blew the entire lid off Lucas's temper. The principal kept his quiet demeanor, but he told a terrified five-year-old child with an undiagnosed neurodevelopmental disorder to either come with him to his office or he would call the police. Lucas screamed in terror, threw the desk over in the hallway, and attempted to run out the door. The assistant teacher caught up to him, grabbed him by the waist, and picked the boy up to carry him to the principal's office. I heard the child screaming until he was out of earshot. I imagine he screamed his entire way to the principal's office, as his eyes were still bloodshot and watery when he was returned to class later that day.

Don't get me wrong. I don't think Lucas was tortured in the principal's office, but I thought the situation could have been handled a lot better. I also have to respect that I was an outsider in that situation, a casual observer. I think we can all agree that in that moment, Lucas was a difficult student. That didn't really change during my time as an observer either. What changed was how the teachers managed him. While I do hope Lucas gets the help and services he needs, let's shift from his example to talk about how you can manage difficult situations and challenging students.

What NOT to Do [lv]

This is a great place to start because while we have a list of responses to bad behavior that many of us use intuitively, when it comes to challenging students, we want to try and curb some intuitive responses and behaviors in ourselves.

<u>Don't Argue</u>: While it may seem like you're trying to hold your student accountable for their actions, arguing doesn't do that. Arguing turns the situation into a "he said, she said," and gives the student the mistaken idea they are somehow on an equal footing with you. They are not. If you are willing to arguing with difficult students, you will soon find yourself arguing with all of your students.

<u>Don't Interrogate</u>: This is another attempt at accountability gone wrong. It's pretty normal for teachers to grill, or at least lightly singe, their students by demanding a response to questions. Where have you been? Why isn't your homework done? Why are you standing in the hall when you're supposed to be in class? But when you interrogate your students in this manner, it doesn't have the desired effect of helping the student be more accountable for their actions. It creates resentment, which has never, as far as I'm

aware, been an ingredient for good behavior management.

Don't Lecture, Scold, or Yell: Just as I mentioned in the previous chapter, if your words do not have an educational purpose, bite your tongue. There will undoubtedly be times when you are overwhelmed, overworked, under-supported, and at the end of your rope. You might be all of the above on the same day. Yet you are a professional, and if your words are going to belittle and lecture and scold your class or even one student, these words will have a long-term damaging effect. If you need a break from your class, it's time for them to put their heads downs. Turn off the lights and put on a video for ten minutes. Is that the best use of educational time? No, but it buys you some time to take deep breaths and refocus. You could all probably use the same refresher period.

<u>Don't Ignore Misbehavior</u>: Consistency is key. When it comes to managing student behavior, especially in a classroom setting, there will always be someone watching. You can't let Robbie get away with the same behavior you regularly correct Margot for. That's not consistent. In your mind you might think Robbie is so well behaved, so one little slip-up isn't a big deal. You can bet Margot thinks it's a big deal, and so will other students. You need to be consistent with all your students and treat them uniformly, or you will have students who push and test you to see how much you will let them get away with.

<u>Don't Lose Control</u>: Who is the adult in the room? Who is the professional? When you let your students get under your skin and you react by giving an eye roll, your students know they can get to you. Keep your cool and stay professional in front of them. You can smash a

book or two against your desk when nobody's watching. I know that keeping your cool sometimes requires a superhuman ability, but your future self will feel grateful if you manage to keep the Hulk inside. This being said, make sure to channel all the frustration and stress that accumulates in your body in a productive way. Take boxing classes or do yoga. Meditate. Do whatever helps you to recenter and soothe yourself. Not losing control in your classroom is one form of self-care; losing control in a beloved activity is another one.

Many everyday challenges put you against the students you are trying to help. One of the greatest barriers to learning is fear, fear that you aren't smart enough, you won't give the correct answer, that others will make fun of you for not knowing, or that you don't belong in the program. An educational environment that breeds the types of reactions above is inherently based in fear, fear of reprisal, fear of being gotten over on, fear someone is getting an advantage you are not. The goal should be to create a safe learning space where students are valued for not just what they know, but who they are, who they can become. Where they know that as individuals, they have purpose and are redeemable. When we offer that to our students, we offer a good base for students to thrive, where mistakes are okay because they teach us how to grow, not that we won't amount to anything.

How to Effectively Work with Difficult Students

<u>Define Expectations:</u>[lvi] If you expect your students to abide by certain rules of conduct, you need to be clear with them what those rules are. Better yet, recruit your students to help you draft those rules and their consequences. What are the

rules of behavior we expect from all participants in this class? What happens when you don't bring your work in on time? If you break a rule, what will be the consequences? Remember to display your list in your classroom and then hold students accountable to their code of conduct.

<u>Justify Your Expectations</u>:[lvii] It's not enough to just list out what the expectations are; you need to explain why the expectations exist in the first place. Did your parent ever give you such priceless reasons of "because I said so," or "do as I say, not as I do?" I bet those reasons didn't go over so well when you were growing up, and they won't be a hit in your classroom either. You need to be able to let students know that rules and policies are set in place to keep everyone safe and enhance learning. When we follow the rules and aren't disruptive, we get more done and that benefits all of us.

<u>Enforce Your Expectations</u>:[lviii] This can be one of the harder parts of working with the rules: being the authority figure. As mentioned, you have to enforce the rules consistently and fairly. It's important to understand that rules are rules and they should be explained and described as such. You should refrain from describing bad conduct as behavior you don't "like" to see and good behavior as something you "want" to see.

For instance: Jane is stomping her feet and throwing rocks on the playground. You respond, "I don't like that behavior, Jane." By describing her actions in this manner, you imply that Jane's behavior is meant to make you happy. This removes the true justification behind the rule enforcement. Instead, you might say, "Jane, throwing rocks on the playground isn't safe because you could hit a friend and really hurt them. Remember we don't throw things. That's one of our class rules."

Make A Choice:[(lix)] When you wake up each day, you make a choice about your attitude and who you are going to be that day. You can choose to be angry and bitter, or you can choose to be happy and put your best efforts out in the world. You can make this same kind of choice when it comes to working with difficult students. Whether you realize it or not, over time, working with difficult learners wears on you. This emotional fatigue, in turn, impacts how you approach them. While you may not say or do anything overtly to indicate that working with a student is stressful and is wearing you down, students have their own intuitive nature. They can pick up how you're feeling about them based on your closed-off body language and tight smile. Maybe you don't ask them the same kinds of questions that you ask other students. Maybe this student had a previous reputation at your school as a troublemaker, and you never really gave them a chance to prove themselves.

How are you going to deal with that? Ultimately, it is up to you to make the choice to actively like your student. Forgive this student's past behavior and make a conscious decision to see the best in them. Focus on how can you help every single student achieve—including the black sheep. Keep your body language open and your smile genuine. Encourage your students to give their best by giving your best first. Very few educators are willing to take on the most difficult students in this way. If you dare opening your heart to make this commitment to your student, you may find they are resilient and are willing to try for you in a way they are not willing for other educators. I encourage you to make this choice for yourself and your challenging student. You might be the only person in that child's life who doesn't write them off.

Be Influential:[lx] When you work with difficult students, it's not enough to offer encouragement, wisdom, and hope. With these students it often seems like your words go unheard and your advice unheeded. To make a difference with this group, you need to garner a certain amount of influence. You can do this by sticking to a few simple rules.

1. Don't create friction. You do this by not doing most of the things we discussed at the beginning of the chapter. Every time you interrogate, yell, or glare at a challenging student, it severs the lines of communication with them and damages any influence you could hope to have.

2. Be consistent. If you want to build a relationship with the problem students,

don't let anyone off the hook. You might think you'll let some things slide here and there and you'll be seen as the easygoing, cool teacher. What this behavior tells your students is that you can't be trusted. That you can't stand your ground. Be consistent all day every day and your students will eventually realize you can be taken at your word, and that level of trust will hopefully blossom into influence.

3. Be kind—no strings attached. A small compliment, random chitchat, asking about an interest goes a long way. Because you don't demand anything in return, it can help the student view you differently than other adults. That's pretty powerful.

The goal of gaining influence with problem students is that when you say something, when you have advice and wisdom that needs to be heeded, these students will be more likely to listen and take your words to heart because you have *influence* in their life. Who knows, you might just change the entire trajectory of their life by being an educator they can trust.

Don't Praise a Good Day:[lxi] It's the end of the day and your difficult student has behaved magnificently. All you want to do is rush over in the last few minutes of class and give them a high five and let them pick a treat from the prize box. And maybe give them a certificate to commemorate this great day as an encouragement so they do it all over again tomorrow. Despite your best intentions, this isn't the best idea. Good behavior is a reward all in itself. When you give students rewards for normal behavior, they come to expect that external reward. What happens when this student behaves as she is expected to every day—will you have to reward them daily? That's just it, though. Normal behavior is part of community expectations, and individuals don't receive rewards for behaving within those expectations. They get the benefit of being members of the community, and that is reward enough. While outstanding achievement should be praised and even rewarded, basics should be acknowledged internally only.

Additionally, difficult students who make changes of their own volition experience a sense of empowerment. Their motivation isn't purchased by the promise of a treat or a certificate. They were intrinsically motivated to make a change, and they earned the success of their work. That satisfaction is something that cannot be bought. This doesn't mean you need to ignore the fact your difficult student had a good day. Just treat them like every other student in your class. Recognize their behavior in the same way you would any other student. For young children, this might be reporting to parents on a behavior chart in a folder they take home each day. Older students may not receive any recognition at all. Maybe share a brief nod and smile as they walk out of class just to let them know you noticed.

Working with challenging students can be the most draining and yet most rewarding experience you have as an educator. These students can be rude, frustrating, talented, funny, gifted, and yet work themselves into unnecessary difficulty. Sometimes it's maddening, but as an educator, when you have those breakthroughs and your students achieve their goals, the joy of watching them succeed is almost as momentous as when *you* succeed. There are almost no words for how much satisfaction it can give to work with a difficult student and watch them flourish and grow.

However, unfortunately this success story isn't always going to happen. It's important that as an educator you find ways to cope with that. Channel your energy into something you love. Find a network of teachers who can serve as a support group. Develop a hobby that allows you to create something beautiful. Whatever it is, let it be something that is for you, and something that allows you to turn your mind off from teaching, if just for a while.

Conclusion

Teaching is a skill and profession that requires creative problem solving, excellent communication skills, working with difficult students who can sometimes create devastating challenges, and not having all the support you need administratively or monetarily to do the things you need to perform your job in the best possible way. On top of that, in the age of COVID, many people who just aren't cut out for it have become impromptu educators trying to teach their kids a grade level and maintain full-time employment. It's very well possible that we may emerge from the global COVID-19 pandemic to discover the educational landscape has changed dramatically. That has yet to be determined.

What we do know is that high-quality educators are needed more than ever. This book presented many of the personal skills needed to become a top-quality educator working with students in a variety of settings. How we approach teaching is just as important as designing a syllabus or a rubric.

I hope this book has given you the skills and resources you need to think about when it comes to the kind of educator you want to be. The practices presented here are some that anyone can implement in their classroom, with their family, in a community learning center, or in corporate training settings. You don't have to use them all at once, just as you see fit for your particular needs. The important part for you to realize is that while you may not be a teacher by trade, you are an educator for life.

About the Author

Gunnar "Gun" Stevenson is a mechanical engineer who veered into academic education. He has spent years researching human behavior through the lens of anthropology, psychology, political science, economics, and pedagogy.

Gun uses his creativity and sharp deductive skills to share lessons from his research and teaching experience in an approachable way. His goal is to help people become more effective educators by tailoring his innovative teaching philosophy to the needs of individual learners.

Don't forget to download your Free Essential Teaching Theories Booklet from www.gunstevenson.com!

Citations

8 Tips to Teach Effectively in Classroom. (2015, June 18). Fedena. https://fedena.com/blog/2015/06/8-tips-to-teach-effectively-in-classroom.html.

20 Ways to Provide Effective Feedback for Learning. (2018, December 7). Teachthought. https://www.teachthought.com/pedagogy/20-ways-to-provide-effective-feedback-for-learning/.

Active Learning Strategies. (n.d.). Center for Excellence in Teaching and Learning at the University of Connecticut. Retrieved December 3, 2020, from https://cetl.uconn.edu/active-learning-strategies/.

Augustyn, A. (n.d.). *The 10 Greatest Basketball Players of All Time.* Britannica. Retrieved December 3, 2020, from https://www.britannica.com/list/the-10-greatest-basketball-players-of-all-time.

Bruzzese, A. (2020, October 2). *6 Ways to Clearly Communicate Complex Information.* Quick Base. https://www.quickbase.com/blog/6-ways-to-clearly-communicate-complex-information.

Busch, B. (2016, November 10). *Seven ways to give better feedback to your students.* The Guardian. https://www.theguardian.com/teacher-network/2016/nov/10/seven-ways-to-give-better-feedback-to-your-students.

Cheung, C. (2001, January 1). The use of popular culture as a stimulus to motivate secondary students' English learning in Hong Kong. *ELT Journal, 55*(1), 55-61. https://doi.org/10.1093/elt/55.1.55.

Cherry, K. (2020, May 15). *The Experiential Learning Theory of David Kolb.* Verywellmind. https://www.verywellmind.com/experiential-learning-2795154.

Cicerchia, M. (n.d.). *What motivates students to learn?*. Read and Spell. Retrieved December 3, 2020, from https://www.readandspell.com/us/what-motivates-students-to-learn.

Cox, J. (2019, October 22). *Tips for Handling Difficult Students.* ThoughtCo. https://www.thoughtco.com/tips-on-handling-difficult-students-2081545.

Dodson, A. (2017, May 26). *LeBron James pays heartfelt tribute to Michael Jordan after breaking record.* The Undefeated. https://theundefeated.com/features/lebron-james-pays-tribute-to-michael-jordan-after-breaking-record/.

Effective Communication Tips for the Classroom. (2015, June 1). Ministry of Education, Guyana. https://education.gov.gy/web/index.php/teachers/tips-for-teaching/item/1504-effective-communication-tips-for-the-classroom.

Ferlazzo, L. (2015, March 25). *Strategies for Helping Students Motivate Themselves.* Edutopia.

https://www.edutopia.org/blog/strategies-helping-students-motivate-themselves-larry-ferlazzo

[JayMJ23]. (2006, August 25). *Michael Jordan "Failure" Nike Commercial* [Video]. Youtube. https://www.youtube.com/watch?v=45mMioJ5szc.

Lam, C. (2014, July 5). *11 Habits of an Effective Teacher.* Edutopia. https://www.edutopia.org/discussion/11-habits-effective-teacher.

Linsin, M. (2017, April 29). *A Radical Way to Transform Difficult Students.* Smart Classroom Management. https://www.smartclassroommanagement.com/2017/04/29/a-radical-way-to-transform-difficult-students/.

Linsin, M. (2017, February 18). *How to Get Difficult Students to Listen to You.* Smart Classroom Management. https://www.smartclassroommanagement.com/2017/02/18/how-to-get-difficult-students-to-listen-to-you/.

Linsin, M. (2011, April 23). *The 7 Rules of Handling Difficult Students.* Smart Classroom Management. https://www.smartclassroommanagement.com/2011/04/23/7-rules-of-handling-difficult-students/.

Linsin, M. (2014, January 25). *Why You Shouldn't Respond When A Difficult Student Has A Good Day.* Smart Classroom Management. https://www.smartclassroommanagement.com/2014/01/25/why-you-shouldnt-respond-when-a-difficult-student-has-a-good-day/.

Merriam-Webster. (n.d.). Communication. In *Merriam-Webster.com dictionary.* Retrieved December 3, 2020, from https://www.merriam-webster.com/dictionary/communication.

Office of Medical Education Research and Development. (n.d.). *Active Learning Strategies.* Michigan State University. Retrieved December 3,

2020, from https://omerad.msu.edu/teaching/teaching-strategies/active-learning-strategies.

Prozesky, D. R. (2000). Communication and Effective Teaching. *Community Eye Health Journal, 13*(35), 44-45. https://www.ncbi.nlm.nih.gov/pmc/articles/PMC1705977/.

Ruzic, D. [Illinois EnergyProf]. (2020, August 4). *How to convert a microwave oven into a plasma-generating N-95 respirator decontamination unit* [Video]. Youtube. https://www.youtube.com/watch?v=7gm8QBbFGyM.

Scaffolding. (2015, April 6). The Glossary of Education Reform. https://www.edglossary.org/scaffolding/.

Schelzig, E. (2018, April 3). *Lawmaker cites satirical website to nix hazing bill.* On the Hill. https://onthehill.tnjournal.net/onion-summer/.

Sherrington, T. (2013, February 13). *Great Lessons 6: Explaining.* Teacherhead. https://teacherhead.com/2013/02/13/great-lessons-6-explaining/.

Silver, F. (2018, July 1). *Why Is It Important for Teachers to Have Good Communication Skills?.* Chron. https://work.chron.com/important-teachers-good-communication-skills-10512.html.

Tonkin, T. (2017, March 17). *Three steps to Make Learning Last.* Cornerstone on Demand. https://www.cornerstoneondemand.com/rework/three-steps-make-learning-last.

Top Qualities of an Effective Teacher. (n.d.). The Center for New Designs in Learning and Scholarship at Georgetown University. Retrieved December 3, 2020, from https://cndls.georgetown.edu/atprogram/twl/effective-teacher/.

Udayan, T. (n.d.). *10 Best Free Educational Apps for Students & Kids*. Mindster. Retrieved December 3, 2020, from https://mindster.com/free-educational-apps-students/.

What Motivates Students to learn?. (2017, June 2). Lamar University. https://degree.lamar.edu/articles/education/what-motivates-students-to-learn/.

Other Works

Miss Nelson Is Missing
> https://www.goodreads.com/book/show/147732.Miss_Nelson_Is_Missing_

Disney's *Coco*
> https://www.imdb.com/title/tt2380307/?ref_=fn_al_tt_1

Kindergarten Cop

https://www.imdb.com/title/tt0099938/?r ef =fn al tt 1

The Hollow Crown

https://www.imdb.com/title/tt2262456/?r ef =fn al tt 1

Braveheart

https://www.imdb.com/title/tt0112573/?r ef =fn al tt 1

Elizabeth(1998)

https://www.imdb.com/title/tt0127536/?r ef =fn al tt 1

Lady Jane(1986)

https://www.imdb.com/title/tt0091374/?r ef =fn al tt 1

182

Endnotes

[i] 8 Tips to Teach Effectively in Classroom. (2015, June 18). Fedena. https://fedena.com/blog/2015/06/8-tips-to-teach-effectively-in-classroom.html.

[ii] Lam, C. (2014, July 5). 11 Habits of an Effective Teacher. Edutopia. https://www.edutopia.org/discussion/11-habits-effective-teacher.

[iii] 8 Tips to Teach Effectively in Classroom. (2015, June 18). Fedena. https://fedena.com/blog/2015/06/8-tips-to-teach-effectively-in-classroom.html.

[iv] Top Qualities of an Effective Teacher. (n.d.). The Center for New Designs in Learning and Scholarship at Georgetown University. Retrieved December 3, 2020, from https://cndls.georgetown.edu/atprogram/twl/effective-teacher/.

[v] 8 Tips to Teach Effectively in Classroom. (2015, June 18). Fedena. https://fedena.com/blog/2015/06/8-tips-to-teach-effectively-in-classroom.html.

[vi] Lam, C. (2014, July 5). 11 Habits of an Effective Teacher. Edutopia. https://www.edutopia.org/discussion/11-habits-effective-teacher.

[vii] Top Qualities of an Effective Teacher. (n.d.). The Center for New Designs in Learning and Scholarship at Georgetown University. Retrieved December 3, 2020, from

https://cndls.georgetown.edu/atprogram/twl/effective-teacher/.

viii 8 Tips to Teach Effectively in Classroom. (2015, June 18). Fedena. https://fedena.com/blog/2015/06/8-tips-to-teach-effectively-in-classroom.html.

ix 8 Tips to Teach Effectively in Classroom. (2015, June 18). Fedena. https://fedena.com/blog/2015/06/8-tips-to-teach-effectively-in-classroom.html.

x Lam, C. (2014, July 5). 11 Habits of an Effective Teacher. Edutopia. https://www.edutopia.org/discussion/11-habits-effective-teacher.

xi Top Qualities of an Effective Teacher. (n.d.). The Center for New Designs in Learning and Scholarship at Georgetown University. Retrieved December 3, 2020, from https://cndls.georgetown.edu/atprogram/twl/effective-teacher/.

xii [JayMJ23]. (2006, August 25). Michael Jordan "Failure" Nike Commercial [Video]. Youtube. https://www.youtube.com/watch?v=45mMioJ5szc.

xiii Augustyn, A. (n.d.). The 10 Greatest Basketball Players of All Time. Britannica. Retrieved December 3, 2020, from https://www.britannica.com/list/the-10-greatest-basketball-players-of-all-time.

xiv Dodson, A. (2017, May 26). LeBron James pays heartfelt tribute to Michael Jordan after breaking record. The Undefeated. https://theundefeated.com/features/lebron-james-pays-tribute-to-michael-jordan-after-breaking-record/.

xv Cicerchia, M. (n.d.). What motivates students to learn?. Read and Spell. Retrieved December 3, 2020, from https://www.readandspell.com/us/what-motivates-students-to-learn.

xvi Ruzic, D. [Illinois EnergyProf]. (2020, August 4). How to convert a microwave oven into a plasma-generating N-95 respirator decontamination unit [Video]. Youtube. https://www.youtube.com/watch?v=7gm8QBbFGyM.

[xvii] Cicerchia, M. (n.d.). What motivates students to learn?. Read and Spell. Retrieved December 3, 2020, from https://www.readandspell.com/us/what-motivates-students-to-learn.

[xviii] Ferlazzo, L. (2015, March 25). Strategies for Helping Students Motivate Themselves. Edutopia. https://www.edutopia.org/blog/strategies-helping-students-motivate-themselves-larry-ferlazzo

[xix] Cicerchia, M. (n.d.). What motivates students to learn?. Read and Spell. Retrieved December 3, 2020, from https://www.readandspell.com/us/what-motivates-students-to-learn.

[xx] Cicerchia, M. (n.d.). What motivates students to learn?. Read and Spell. Retrieved December 3, 2020, from https://www.readandspell.com/us/what-motivates-students-to-learn.

[xxi] Cheung, C. (2001, January 1). The use of popular culture as a stimulus to motivate secondary students' English learning in Hong Kong. ELT Journal, 55(1), 55-61. https://doi.org/10.1093/elt/55.1.55.

[xxii] Ferlazzo, L. (2015, March 25). Strategies for Helping Students Motivate Themselves. Edutopia. https://www.edutopia.org/blog/strategies-helping-students-motivate-themselves-larry-ferlazzo

[xxiii] What Motivates Students to learn?. (2017, June 2). Lamar University. https://degree.lamar.edu/articles/education/what-motivates-students-to-learn/.

[xxiv] Merriam-Webster. (n.d.). Communication. In Merriam-Webster.com dictionary. Retrieved December 3, 2020, from https://www.merriam-webster.com/dictionary/communication.

185

[xxv] Prozesky, D. R. (2000). Communication and Effective
Teaching. Community Eye Health Journal, 13(35), 44-45.
https://www.ncbi.nlm.nih.gov/pmc/articles/PMC1705977/.
[xxvi] Prozesky, D. R. (2000). Communication and Effective
Teaching. Community Eye Health Journal, 13(35), 44-45.
https://www.ncbi.nlm.nih.gov/pmc/articles/PMC1705977/.
[xxvii] Prozesky, D. R. (2000). Communication and Effective
Teaching. Community Eye Health Journal, 13(35), 44-45.
https://www.ncbi.nlm.nih.gov/pmc/articles/PMC1705977/.
[xxviii] Prozesky, D. R. (2000). Communication and Effective
Teaching. Community Eye Health Journal, 13(35), 44-45.
https://www.ncbi.nlm.nih.gov/pmc/articles/PMC1705977/.
[xxix] Prozesky, D. R. (2000). Communication and Effective
Teaching. Community Eye Health Journal, 13(35), 44-45.
https://www.ncbi.nlm.nih.gov/pmc/articles/PMC1705977/.
[xxx] Prozesky, D. R. (2000). Communication and Effective
Teaching. Community Eye Health Journal, 13(35), 44-45.
https://www.ncbi.nlm.nih.gov/pmc/articles/PMC1705977/.
[xxxi] Prozesky, D. R. (2000). Communication and Effective
Teaching. Community Eye Health Journal, 13(35), 44-45.
https://www.ncbi.nlm.nih.gov/pmc/articles/PMC1705977/.
[xxxii] Prozesky, D. R. (2000). Communication and Effective
Teaching. Community Eye Health Journal, 13(35), 44-45.
https://www.ncbi.nlm.nih.gov/pmc/articles/PMC1705977/.
[xxxiii] Prozesky, D. R. (2000). Communication and Effective
Teaching. Community Eye Health Journal, 13(35), 44-45.
https://www.ncbi.nlm.nih.gov/pmc/articles/PMC1705977/.
[xxxiv] Silver, F. (2018, July 1). Why Is It Important for Teachers
to Have Good Communication Skills?. Chron.
https://work.chron.com/important-teachers-good-
communication-skills-10512.html.
[xxxv] Silver, F. (2018, July 1). Why Is It Important for Teachers
to Have Good Communication Skills?. Chron.
https://work.chron.com/important-teachers-good-
communication-skills-10512.html.

[xxxvi] Merriam-Webster. (n.d.). Communication. In Merriam-Webster.com dictionary. Retrieved December 3, 2020, from https://www.merriam-webster.com/dictionary/communication.

[xxxvii] Effective Communication Tips for the Classroom. (2015, June 1). Ministry of Education, Guyana. https://education.gov.gy/web/index.php/teachers/tips-for-teaching/item/1504-effective-communication-tips-for-the-classroom.

[xxxviii] Sherrington, T. (2013, February 13). Great Lessons 6: Explaining. Teacherhead. https://teacherhead.com/2013/02/13/great-lessons-6-explaining/.

[xxxix] Bruzzese, A. (2020, October 2). 6 Ways to Clearly Communicate Complex Information. Quick Base. https://www.quickbase.com/blog/6-ways-to-clearly-communicate-complex-information.

[xl] Bruzzese, A. (2020, October 2). 6 Ways to Clearly Communicate Complex Information. Quick Base. https://www.quickbase.com/blog/6-ways-to-clearly-communicate-complex-information.

[xli] Bruzzese, A. (2020, October 2). 6 Ways to Clearly Communicate Complex Information. Quick Base. https://www.quickbase.com/blog/6-ways-to-clearly-communicate-complex-information.

[xlii] Scaffolding. (2015, April 6). The Glossary of Education Reform. https://www.edglossary.org/scaffolding/.

[xliii] Sherrington, T. (2013, February 13). Great Lessons 6: Explaining. Teacherhead. https://teacherhead.com/2013/02/13/great-lessons-6-explaining/.

[xliv] Bruzzese, A. (2020, October 2). 6 Ways to Clearly Communicate Complex Information. Quick Base. https://www.quickbase.com/blog/6-ways-to-clearly-communicate-complex-information.

[xlv] Active Learning Strategies. (n.d.). Center for Excellence in Teaching and Learning at the University of Connecticut. Retrieved December 3, 2020, from https://cetl.uconn.edu/active-learning-strategies/.
[xlvi] Office of Medical Education Research and Development. (n.d.). Active Learning Strategies. Michigan State University. Retrieved December 3, 2020, from https://omerad.msu.edu/teaching/teaching-strategies/active-learning-strategies.
[xlvii] Office of Medical Education Research and Development. (n.d.). Active Learning Strategies. Michigan State University. Retrieved December 3, 2020, from https://omerad.msu.edu/teaching/teaching-strategies/active-learning-strategies.
[xlviii] Baines, Lawrence. A teacher's guide to multisensory learning : improving literacy by engaging the senses. United States: Association for Supervision and Curriculum Development, 2008.
[xlix] Schelzig, E. (2018, April 3). Lawmaker cites satirical website to nix hazing bill. On the Hill. https://onthehill.tnjournal.net/onion-summer/.
[l] Cherry, K. (2020, May 15). The Experiential Learning Theory of David Kolb. Verywellmind. https://www.verywellmind.com/experiential-learning-2795154.
[li] Tonkin, T. (2017, March 17). Three steps to Make Learning Last. Cornerstone on Demand. https://www.cornerstoneondemand.com/rework/three-steps-make-learning-last.
[lii] Udayan, T. (n.d.). 10 Best Free Educational Apps for Students & Kids. Mindster. Retrieved December 3, 2020, from https://mindster.com/free-educational-apps-students/.
[liii] 20 Ways to Provide Effective Feedback for Learning. (2018, December 7). Teachthought.

https://www.teachthought.com/pedagogy/20-ways-to-provide-effective-feedback-for-learning/.

[liv] Busch, B. (2016, November 10). Seven ways to give better feedback to your students. The Guardian. https://www.theguardian.com/teacher-network/2016/nov/10/seven-ways-to-give-better-feedback-to-your-students.

[lv] Linsin, M. (2011, April 23). The 7 Rules of Handling Difficult Students. Smart Classroom Management. https://www.smartclassroommanagement.com/2011/04/23/7-rules-of-handling-difficult-students/.

[lvi] Cox, J. (2019, October 22). Tips for Handling Difficult Students. ThoughtCo. https://www.thoughtco.com/tips-on-handling-difficult-students-2081545.

[lvii] Cox, J. (2019, October 22). Tips for Handling Difficult Students. ThoughtCo. https://www.thoughtco.com/tips-on-handling-difficult-students-2081545.

[lviii] Cox, J. (2019, October 22). Tips for Handling Difficult Students. ThoughtCo. https://www.thoughtco.com/tips-on-handling-difficult-students-2081545.

[lix] Linsin, M. (2017, April 29). A Radical Way to Transform Difficult Students. Smart Classroom Management. https://www.smartclassroommanagement.com/2017/04/29/a-radical-way-to-transform-difficult-students/.

[lx] Linsin, M. (2017, February 18). How to Get Difficult Students to Listen to You. Smart Classroom Management. https://www.smartclassroommanagement.com/2017/02/18/how-to-get-difficult-students-to-listen-to-you/.

[lxi] Linsin, M. (2014, January 25). Why You Shouldn't Respond When A Difficult Student Has A Good Day. Smart Classroom Management. https://www.smartclassroommanagement.com/2014/01/25/why-you-shouldnt-respond-when-a-difficult-student-has-a-good-day/.

Printed in Great Britain
by Amazon